TOMMY COOPER'S
Mirth, Magic & Mischief

Best Wishes
Tommy Cooper
"Almost a Magician"

Also by John Fisher

Funny Way to be a Hero
The Magic of Lewis Carroll
Call Them Irreplaceable
George Formby: The Ukulele Man
Never Give a Sucker an Even Break
Paul Daniels & the Story of Magic
Body Magic
Cardini: The Suave Deceiver
Tommy Cooper: Always Leave Them Laughing
Tony Hancock: The Definitive Biography
The Tommy Cooper Joke Book

TOMMY COOPER'S MIRTH, MAGIC & MISCHIEF

JOHN FISHER

preface

Published by Preface 2010

10 9 8 7 6 5 4 3 2 1

Copyright © John Fisher and the Tommy Cooper Estate, 2010

John Fisher has asserted his right to be identified as the author
of this work under the Copyright, Designs and Patents Act 1988

First published in Great Britain in 2010 by Preface Publishing
20 Vauxhall Bridge Road
London, SW1V 2SA

An imprint of The Random House Group Limited

www.rbooks.co.uk
www.prefacepublishing.co.uk

Addresses for companies within The Random House Group Limited
can be found at www.randomhouse.co.uk

The Random House Group Limited Reg. No. 954009

A CIP catalogue record for this book is available from the British Library

ISBN 978 1 84809 455 0

Designed & illustrated by Andy Spence Design
www.andyspence.co.uk

Printed and bound in India by Replika Press Pvt. Ltd.

Lenticular artwork by Holovision

For Madi –
'me too!'
– with love

CONTENTS

CONTENTS

CONTENTS

CONTENTS

Bending Spoon

Tricks & Gags for
Palladium

Collapsible Tables.

1. Collapsible Tables.
2. ? Blindfold Trick wa
3. Dove Pan. Chick
4. Gun.
5. Cigarettes Bo

Magic Act

1. Rabbit Table & H
2. Skeleton Rabbit.
3. Four Aces ?
4. Die Box.
5. Egg Bag.
6. 3 in one Rope with
   "Grater.
7. Finger Chopper.
8. Flat Rabbit
9. Potato Pot Peeler

Tricks in Pocket

1. Knots Hydraf & Hole.
2. Thimble
3. Heavy Cards
4. Sponge Balls.
5. Cards & Gum.
6. Chase the Ace.
7. Rope w/ sleeve (or in Trousers)
8. Burning Heleif
9. Egg Bag — Silk
10. Cigar &
11. Card
12. Cycle
13. Carry
14. Trick

T.V. Tricks

Timing! — Saw
gag := I shall never
forget the last time
I did that trick — and
I have two half sisters
to prove it!!!... into! —
Paper Bag, will now
produce a dove higher
I always lit that bag
to hand!! into! —

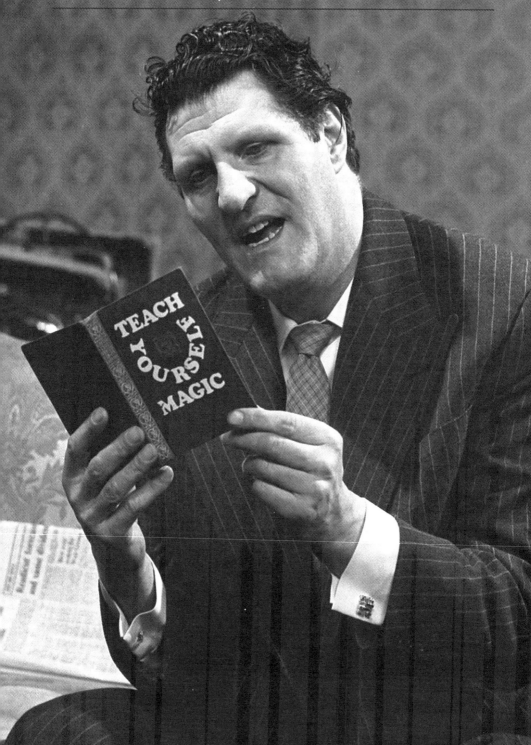

'Magic ... It's Like Christmas!'

An introduction by John Fisher

Tommy Cooper was mad about magic. He was also pretty good at it, far more than his reputation as the world's most helpless hocus-pocus man would suggest. An ideal day for Cooper during the early part of his career would have been to rise at midday, embark upon the rounds of the London magic depots where his presence and custom were always welcomed, move on to a gathering of one of the several magic clubs that flourished in London in those days, possibly trying out some new material on his pals in the process, and then only when others were contemplating bedtime to progress to the reality of work – late-night cabaret at one of the nightclubs where in those days turns, rather than turntables, provided the entertainment on offer.

His obsession with the gadgets and gizmos of his trade is typified by a story told by Martin Breese, a respected purveyor of apparatus to the magical fraternity. One morning Tommy came on the phone to order several of the most expensive tricks from Martin's most recent catalogue. He also asked if the order could be rushed through and delivered without delay. When Martin asked for the address, the voice replied, *'Charing Cross Hospital.'* It was never difficult to impersonate Tommy Cooper over the phone. Martin sensed a joke and hung up. But a few seconds later a niggling doubt found him ringing the hospital to check. Tommy had indeed been admitted as a patient. Martin was put through to the ward. *'Well, can you deliver?'* asked Cooper. A short cab ride later Breese was at the hospital, only to discover Tommy in a wheelchair outside an operating theatre awaiting minor foot surgery. Amid a flurry of string and brown paper, parcels were opened and props examined until it was time to wave goodbye to the Goliath of comedy as he was wheeled into the operating theatre with a mountain of the latest miracles spilling over his lap.

Tommy first caught the bug one Christmas when he was given a box of tricks by his aunt Lucy. He was no more than seven or eight at the time. In his own words, *'I took to magic straight away. All my spending money went on new tricks and all the time I could spare went on practising them.'* His entrée to a wider world of wonder was provided by the back pages of comics like *Wizard* and *Rover*. These carried advertisements for Ellisdons, the High Holborn firm that proclaimed itself 'the largest mail order house in the world for jokes, magic and novelties.' To peruse the pages of the company's catalogues today is to be transported back into a paper paradise of mirth and mystery, hilarity and bewilderment, do-it-yourself spectacle and tinsel razzamatazz.

No child thus enticed would ever again have time for playing cowboys and Indians, collecting cigarette cards, or constructing cranes out of Meccano sets. Here could be found the exoticism of the Arabian Vase illusion, the Hindu Folding Paper Mystery and the Chinese Linking Rings, alongside – albeit playing to baser instincts – Exploding Cigars, Squirting Finger Rings and the Window-Smashing Joke. Once through its doors, Tommy never left this world behind. Other magicians grew out of childhood to become more sophisticated in attitude and demeanour, method and effect, but the pervading ethos of what would become the Cooper act is contained in the Aladdin's cave of these pages. Many years later, when the Ellisdons store was modernised and reopened, Tommy, now a major star and a national figure, was invited along to perform the opening ceremony. He must have been in seventh heaven.

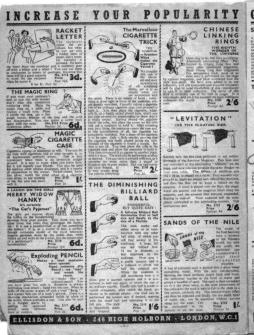

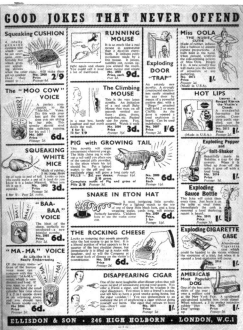

The excitement he experienced when as a boy he waited for the postman to deliver the latest package never left him. In later life he used to acquire many of his props from the Supreme Magic Company in the unlikely location of Bideford, a small coastal town in North Devon. As each new sales list appeared, Tommy would phone his requirements through to the owner, a jovial wizard known throughout the conjuring trade as simply Edwin the Magician. The order was usually the same – *'Send one of everything!'* – to which Edwin would point out that Tommy had several of the items already or that possibly some of them were not suitable for his presentation. Tommy would reply, *'Never mind! Send them anyway. I'm just a big kid and it's like Christmas when I get your parcels!'* The answer contained the key to what made him successful as both a magician and a funny man. He never lost that sense of childish wonder – that of the kid in the candy store, no less – with which every member of his audience could identify. To watch recordings of him now more than twenty-five years after his premature death on live television in the spring of 1984, one sees that his tricks were like toys, his jokes like riddles, and his whole demeanour indicative of the spirit of play. He brought out the child in everyone who watched him and in all those he met.

Away from the theatres and television studios, his pockets always bulged with tricks. No opportunity would be lost to try out the latest on family or friends. According to his wife, Gwen – or 'Dove', as he called her – he even practised card tricks in the lavatory. When he went on tour he travelled with far more apparatus than he needed for his standard act. The average count was around seventeen bags and cases full of magic paraphernalia. He used to say it resembled a small circus: *'That's why I always have two rooms in a hotel. I use the sitting room as the practice room. I love what I'm doing, so when I try something new and it goes well, that's a great tonic for me. It's what I'm most concerned about.'* In truth, most of what he acquired was for his own fascination and never performed in public.

The expensive holidays that came with his success invariably took him and his family to New York or Las Vegas where – while Gwen lounged by the pool

Worlds Tallest

Photo Made Atop Empire State Building, **New York**

1,472 feet,
102 stories

– his days would be spent in the magic shops, while evenings would be dedicated to tracking down all the magic acts performing in town. He loved the company of other magicians, providing each other as they do with an informal masonry to rival the members of any entertainment group. British entertainer Frankie Vaughan recalled the difficulty he once had in getting to his own dressing room in a theatre they were playing together. The corridor was blocked by a long queue of men waiting to get into Tommy's room. They were all amateur magicians wanting to show him their tricks. But Cooper was nothing if not democratic. He was proud of his friendship with arguably the two top straight magicians of the day, the suave American prestidigitator Channing Pollock and the tantalising television wizard Robert Harbin. Deep down he secretly aspired to their elegance and ingenuity, but he was savvy enough to accept that he had found the perfect means of expression for himself and that in public any route that veered away from the apparently burlesque approach would be anathema to his career. An early teenage mishap with a trick involving a bottle of milk had shown the way: *'The stage was swimming with milk. I dropped my wand. I did everything wrong. But the audience loved it. The more I panicked and made a mess of everything, the more they laughed. I came off and cried, but five minutes later I could still hear the sound of the laughter in my ears and was thinking maybe there's a living to be made here.'*

Once he emerged from the services into full-time show business after the Second World War, Cooper quickly developed the ability to discern what material was right for his act and what he could indulge as a hobby. When it came to the former, he knew where he could rely for sound advice in this regard. Of all the magical entrepreneurs of the fifties and sixties the one who had probably the biggest input into the Cooper career was Harry Stanley, whose 'Unique' Magic Studio – situated over the years at a string of addresses throughout Soho – would be as likely a place to find Tommy as anywhere during the daytime. Here all the top pros convened and to Tommy it was home from home. Stanley had a wider grasp of life, of show business and of what was commercial than most magicians. He had toured the world as a musician with Jack Hylton's Band in the thirties and become a confidante of many non-magical entertainers. Even when Tommy was unknown, Stanley had been happy to spread the name by using the Cooper endorsement in his ads. Once Tommy became a household name, the inclusion of a trick from 'Unique' or any of the other magic dealers in one of his television shows would result in increased sales to the many amateur magicians watching. Tommy often dragged his close friend, the comedian Eric Sykes, with him on these magic-shop excursions. As Eric has indicated, many of the owners were so pleased to give him the latest novelty off their shelves that money seldom changed hands.

TOMMY COOPER in "Sunday Night at the London Palladium", featuring our **SUCKER**

COLOUR CHANGING SILK

● **ACKNOWLEDGED TO BE THE GREATEST COMEDY SILK CHANGE EVER DEVISED !**

A Red Silk is passed through the fist to emerge Green. Performer "explains" how it is done . . and shows that he has TWO Silks . . one Red and the other Green. Warning them of the necessity of keeping one carefully concealed, he demonstrates how the change is made . . BUT . . upon opening his hand to show the "concealed" Silk . . it just isn't there! It has **Completely Vanished !** Then, passing the Red Silk once again through the previously shown empty fist . . it emerges **Green !** Both hands are completely EMPTY.

Words cannot adequately describe the brilliance of the routine . . it is a 100% applause getter ! Ask any magician who has seen it ! It is not a "self-working" effect, but with a very modest amount of practice, you will have an item that you will never leave out of your programme. Suitable for Drawing Room, Platform or Stage . . ideal for Compere, First-Class Practical Magic. Complete with all apparatus and silks necessary, nothing else required. Instructions and routine fully illustrated.

Price **22/6** postage 1/-   U.S.A. **$5.00.**

● **AS PERFORMED BY TOMMY COOPER ON T.V**

The Ever Changing Giant Pip Card Everyone in TALKING ABOUT ! ! ! ! !

A GREAT SUCCESS THE WORLD OVER . . this is the **TOPS IN ENTERTAINMENT !** A giant card has first 6 spots, then 3, then 4, then 1. Unfortunately (?) the magician makes a **mistake,** and audience see how the changing effect is brought about. Performer further assists them by explaining exactly **HOW** the trick is done . . but their eyes **Pop,** when suddenly, the card has 6 Spots, 4 spots, 3 spots, 1 spot . . and finally **EIGHT SPOTS !** It's a real **EYE-POPPER** that is CERTAIN to get the LAUGHS ! No flaps. . . **EASY TO DO** . . you can perform this **RIGHT AWAY.**

Price **15/-** postage 1/-   U.S.A. **$3.00.**

UNIQUE   "PLAYING"   CARDS

BY SPECIAL REQUEST I bring back one of our old favourites. Many years ago I sold the first one to TOMMY COOPER and he, and lots of my customers, had plenty of fun with it . . it's a grand gag! You show a pack of cards and say . . "People often ask why these are called **"Playing Cards".** Well, this is why . ." and you put the cards to your mouth and produce MUSIC from them!!! It brings a really **BIG LAUGH.**

Price **6/-** postage 1/-   U.S.A. **$1.50.**

● THE BIGGEST LAUGH with GIANT SIZE CARDS . . . . .
That COMEDY CLASSIC . . . .

"THE FOUR ICES"

The CLIMAX of this great NOVELTY effect is so strong and unexpected that it simply MUST get ROARS OF LAUGHTER from any type of audience . . . and I guarantee that they will remember it long after the "clever stuff".

The effect is that of a normal **Giant Four Ace Routine** . . that is Four Aces are displayed . . each covered with three indifferent cards. One heap is chosen and placed into a large envelope. The remaining three Aces are now caused to **vanish** . . one after another.

The cards in the envelope are removed . . and they are now seen to be **Four Aces** . . but . . with a **difference** . . and **what a difference** . . it will make any audience **howl with laughter!**

EASY TO DO . . NO SLEIGHT OF HAND . . Complete with **giant cards** . . **routine** and **patter** . . everything necessary to do this grand novelty trick RIGHT AWAY.

Price   25/-   post 1/-   U.S.A. $5.00.

● ONE OF THE GREATEST COMEDY PROPS. OF ALL TIME!

UNIQUE

"LEGS TABLE"

(YIMKA)

Laughs . . and the getting of them, provide one of the biggest headaches in show business. A comedy effect which scores heavily at ONE show, can flop completely in the next! To get an item which gives GUARANTEED LAUGHS, is worth it's weight in gold! Here is such an item . . . tried and tested, under every condition, and a PROVEN WINNER—EVERY TIME ! ! ! !

EFFECT :   On stage ,there are two tables (the four-legged kind). Wanting to show an effect more intimately, performer picks up one of the tables and advances to the front of the stage . . but . . Horror of Horror's . . one of the front legs DROPS OFF completely! Looking troubled, magician looks nervously around, wondering what to do, then, to his utter consternation . . the OTHER front leg DROPS OFF too! Looking utterly bewildered, he gazes here and there, as if silently appealing for help . . when . . all of a sudden . . WHAM! two legs APPEAR INSTANTLY on the front of the table, they are a shapely pair of **Ladies' Legs** ! He heaves a sigh of relief, puts the table down, and carries on with his normal show! You will "stop the show" with this one. It is such a "natural" that I have seen a member of the audience run up to the stage, to help the "unfortunate magician"! This of course, brings even more, and greater LAUGHS!!!

Price £18.   Carriage Extra.   U.S.A. $75.00.

Never one for half measures, Tommy took the Multiplying Bottles trick to new heights, producing around thirty bottles in the course of his routine, as shown later in this volume.

Today it is impossible to peruse the nostalgia-filled pages of Stanley's catalogues – a grown-up version of the Ellisdons fun-sheets – without Cooper taking centre stage in one's mind's eye. Here are the suspect wooden duck that pecks out the chosen card in what may well be the most surreal card trick ever; the trick where the four aces get confused with the four ices – *'chocolate ice, strawberry ice, vanilla ice and peppermint ice'*; as well as the glass that changes place with the bottle and the bottle that changes place with the glass – *'but the difficult part is to make them go back again!'* – before the magician gets carried away and the whole table is swamped with

bottles. The table that grows legs, the stool that bounces, the playing cards that emit a tune – he made them all his own. The items known in the trade as sucker tricks were of special value to him. The term designates an effect that the magician seemingly explains to his audience, only to show, when he performs the trick a second time, that he has done no such thing. It may be logical to suppose that when a magician changes the colour of a red handkerchief to green, he is actually manipulating not one, but two handkerchiefs. Tommy is content to show us how. Then you wonder how he will get rid of the superfluous red handkerchief, which, against all expectation, disappears completely – unless he truly has changed the colour of the handkerchief from red to green!

More than a quarter of a century after his demise, people continue to ask just how good a magician Tommy Cooper was. He may not have been as digitally dextrous as Pollock or as wittily clever as Harbin, but as Geoffrey Durham, one of today's top wizards, has said, no performer ever expressed himself better through magic. That in itself qualifies him as the most successful British magician in history. Much of his repertoire, as we have seen, constituted strong magic. He kept a happy balance between the out-and-out burlesque items that refused to work and those moments when genuine success cleverly sneaked up on him when he was least expecting it. The two ingredients were important. Had audiences been left to assume that he was really incompetent, they would not only have given him credit for no skill at all, but found it harder to laugh at his failure in the process, although ironically the precision handling and timing that went into a trick that apparently let him down often involved a higher level of skill than performing it correctly.

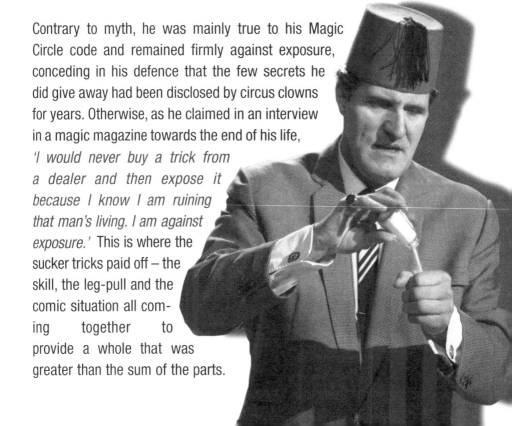

Contrary to myth, he was mainly true to his Magic Circle code and remained firmly against exposure, conceding in his defence that the few secrets he did give away had been disclosed by circus clowns for years. Otherwise, as he claimed in an interview in a magic magazine towards the end of his life, *'I would never buy a trick from a dealer and then expose it because I know I am ruining that man's living. I am against exposure.'* This is where the sucker tricks paid off – the skill, the leg-pull and the comic situation all coming together to provide a whole that was greater than the sum of the parts.

Sucker tricks are, of course, the hocus-pocus equivalent of practical jokes, an area in which he enjoyed himself as much as in the more upfront world of the magical enthusiast. As a boy, inspired by the sneezing powder, whoopee cushions and blackface soap of the Ellisdons emporium, he had gone out of his way to endorse the old Will Rogers adage, 'Everything is funny, as long as it's happening to somebody else.' Many of his gags required elaborate stage management. A favourite involved attaching a length of 'invisible' black thread to a dummy bar of chocolate, placing the chocolate in a prominent position in the school playground, and then retiring with the other end of the thread behind the toilet block where no one could see him. As soon as someone made a grab for the confectionery, Tommy – convulsed with laughter – jerked the thread away and ran off in the opposite direction, leaving his fellow pupil bewildered to say the least.

He remained an inveterate practical joker to the end of his days. Today fans proudly display the pens he gave away with 'Stolen from Tommy Cooper' engraved along the side. Everyone has heard of the infamous tea bag gag. *'Have a drink on me,'* he would reassure a tired taxi driver, tucking an appropriate something into his top pocket. Disappointment turned to laughter (sometimes!) when the unsuspecting cabbie got home to discover a free sample of Tetley's finest. The Cooper home at Chiswick became a domestic minefield where biscuit barrels disgorged monstrous spring snakes, books burst into flames or emitted an electric charge when opened, and a laundry basket once yielded the replica of a bloody

severed hand, cueing a shriek from the Cooper's long-suffering maid, Sheila, that would have curdled the blood of anyone in earshot. And while the members of the household did the best they could to stave off cardiac arrest, Tommy – according to his wife – just laughed and laughed and laughed, lying on the bed with his feet in the air. He had the full measure of the situation though: *'She bloody hates it. Still that's love, isn't it? Funny thing love – it rhymes with Dove – now that is funny!'* A favourite wheeze when waiting for Dove at one of the magic shops was to get the guys there to promise there would be no bad language when she arrived. When she did come through the door, he looked at her and shouted, *'Where the f*ck have you been?'* Gwen gave a coy look that seemed to say, 'Isn't he awful?' while the room rocked with laughter. It was a gag she obviously became used to over the years, a trade-off perhaps for the promise she once successfully exacted from her husband that he would never use dubious humour on stage.

There were times when his sense of mischief sorely tested the best of friendships. He was notorious for phoning his mates in the middle of the night when he got back after a show: *'Hello, Russ. It's Tommy here. I just thought you'd like to know I got back home okay.'* At which point he would hang up. It was four in the morning and he had no thought of going to bed. In fact, Russ or Val or Jimmy or any of his other cronies had no idea he'd been anywhere in the first place. And he was the master of the wind-up. Freddie Starr recalls being taken home by Tommy for a snack and a nightcap in the early hours of the morning. Tommy insisted they should not make a noise between them – for fear of waking the neighbours, for greater fear of disturbing Gwen. They parked a few doors from the house, tiptoed softly up the drive, took off their shoes at the front door, went through the kitchen with the stealth of cat burglars, and kept their voices to the lowest hush. When it came time to go, Freddie gingerly padded his way back to his car down the quiet suburban street while Tommy waited by the front gate. As Starr looked back to wave goodbye, Cooper at the top of his voice roared, *'Now f*ck off – and don't f*cking come back!'* He then slammed the front door with the force of a thunderclap and disappeared inside. It is unlikely that anyone in the vicinity was still asleep after that. One can only guess what Gwen said behind closed doors.

One of my favourite Cooper stories is told by Colin Fox, a respected magician from Leeds, with whom Tommy always spent time together when he played the big Variety Clubs in Batley, Wakefield and the surrounding area. After meeting up in the bar, they would invariably retreat to Tommy's hotel room to swap tricks and trade gossip as only magicians can. Tommy would suggest tea and cakes and phoned room service: *'Send me up a room!'* Needless to say, the line was always funny the way he delivered it. On the occasion in question the meringues brought by the waiter were a week old and shattered the instant they were bitten into. If the truth were known Cooper probably had a secret arrangement with the restaurant to serve him with cakes that were bound to explode. Amends were made with another order for tea and toast. The afternoon progressed with much merriment and an hour or so later Tommy excused himself to go to the bathroom. A few minutes later he emerged wearing nothing but a pair of polka dot jockey shorts and a lady's white bathing cap. He took one look at his friend and said, *'Now, let's be serious for a moment!'*

The scenario sums up the man. Mirth, magic and mischief! This book sets out to evoke the three qualities that combined with a heaven-sent talent to make this fez-capped colossus the magnificent entertainer he was. Hopefully readers will derive as much fun from the tricks and stunts in these pages as Tommy Cooper had as he familiarised himself with the contents of the latest delivery from Ellisdons or Harry Stanley. Tommy was unique, he was incorrigible, and he was arguably the funniest man who ever lived. He was also by far the most popular British magician of all time.

BROWN YOy
BALL IN CUP T
FRYING PAN + fla
& preset match
3 SOLID RINGS
1 PAIR SCISSO
1 PLATE
1 EGG.

1 BLACK F
1 WAITE
1 LARGE FLO
1 RED WAT
1 HACKSAW

'NOW HERE'S A LITTLE TRICK I'D LIKE TO SHOW YOU NOW ...'

This early publicity throwaway shows that Tommy never missed a trick!

A FEW

"MAGIC TRICKS"

—BY—

TOMMY COOPER

"ALMOST A MAGICIAN"

TRY THESE WHEN YOU GET HOME

The **C**RAZY **C**OMIC **C**ONJURER

from the

Television Show

" ITS MAGIC "

A FEW SIMPLE TRICKS BY **TOMMY COOPER**

THE FLYING HEN

Select a large well-fed hen, the colour is immaterial, though black is the best, and place her in a sitting position on some smooth surface. Then over her place a paste-board box eighteen by thirty inches. Pound smartly upon the top of the box with a bone handled table knife for three minutes, and then raise it, when the hen will immediately fly away. This trick can be performed by any person of average intelligence, who gives his whole mind to it.

THE MAGIC STICK

To do this trick properly you will need a knife and a stout hard wood stick some two inches in length. Sharpen the two ends of the stick and try to crush it endways, either between your hands or by sitting upon it. This to your astonishment you will find impossible to do.

THE NAIL TRICK

Take two wrought-iron nails and wire them in the form of a cross. It will then be impossible to swallow them. There is no deception about this.

THE FOUR JACKS

Get a pack of cards with plain white backs. Take out the four Jacks and burn them before the company letting all see the ashes. Now shuffle the cards quickly, and, holding them in the left hand, give them a sharp rap with the knuckles of the right. Then place the cards on the table with the faces down, and defy the company to find the Jacks, not one can do it.

THE ROPE TRICK

Take a piece of tarred rope about fifteen inches in length, cut it carefully in two with a sharp knife and then try to chew the ends together. You can try this as long as you like.

THE MAGIC EGGS

Put two fresh eggs carefully in a green worsted bag. Swing the bag rapidly round your head, hitting it each time against the door post. Then ask the audience if they will have them boiled, fried or scrambled.

Tommy's files reveal that he had other material lined up for subsequent throwaways that never materialised. Here are some of the miracles that he kept up his sleeve.

BEWARE! They are NOT for trying out at home amongst friends!

- Soak a packet of cigarettes in six inches of tepid water. When they are thoroughly wet, ask someone to take out the third cigarette on the left from the top layer. It just cannot be done.

- Empty two tins of wet spaghetti on to your head and stand in the hot sun for fifteen minutes. Then try and comb it. This is magic at its merriest and messiest.

- Invite a member of the audience to come on to the stage. Tell him a funny story and make him laugh. Then stick a pin into some part of his anatomy. When it has penetrated up to half an inch he will stop laughing. That's magic.

- Detach two legs from the body of a dead fly. Blow them into the air and then challenge anyone in the audience to find them. I doubt if they will.

- The following trick requires a large stage. Empty three tons of coal on to a full-sized billiards table. Then ask a member of the audience to pot the pink in the centre pocket. It is not easy.

- Borrow a pair of tortoiseshell spectacles – they must be real tortoiseshell – and break them into small pieces with a small hammer. Drop the pieces out of the window and they will disappear.

- Borrow two dapple-grey racehorses and give one back. Tie three small cans on the tail of the other horse. Then sing a chorus of 'Horsey, Horsey, keep your tail up' and the cans will rise. Then shout, 'Objection' and the cans will drop.

- Invite a lot of friends to your house. When they are all in the drawing room, stand near the door and turn off the lights. Slip quietly out and go to the pictures. When they turn the lights back on, you will not be there.

'FIND THE LADY'

IS THE NAME OF AN AGE-OLD SWINDLE THAT HAS MADE A FORTUNE FOR CROOKED CARD SHARKS. NO ONE EVER FINDS THE QUEEN AND NEITHER WILL YOU – UNLESS YOU PEEK. IN OTHER WORDS, DON'T TURN THE PAGE UNTIL YOU'RE TOLD TO!

The illustration shows the back of five cards. The Queen of Diamonds – the Lady – is in the centre position. You have the publisher's guarantee this is true. The Queen is the card marked 'X'

All you have to do is place a wire paper clip on the edge of that card or – to be exact – over the edge of the page where you can see the card. Once you have clipped the Queen, it is safe to turn the page.

FOOLED AGAIN!

The elusive lady wins once more. If you don't believe it, check it out with real playing cards.

And remember, you can't catch a Queen with a paper clip!

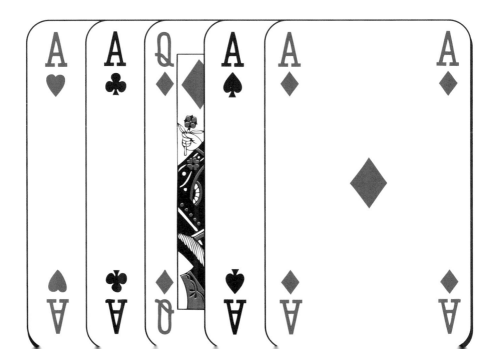

ANIMAL MAGIC

Now in the jungle, you see, there was an elephant and this elephant had a thorn in his foot and this man went across to the elephant and the elephant was like that *(Tommy mimes pain)* – like that he was – and the man got the thorn out, you see, got the thorn out like that and the elephant went like that *(Tommy mimes blank stare)* and he looked at this man, because elephants never forget, do they? Anyway, what have they got to remember? I don't know. And he looked at him and there was a look on his face.

(Tommy mimes look)

And about ten years later this man was in a circus and the elephants were going round like that – all the way round, see, all the way round – and the last elephant stopped and looked at this man and he went like that again, this elephant, and he went slowly towards this man like that and the man went like that and this elephant went right over towards him and put his trunk round him and choked him to death. It was a different elephant! Huh, Huh! Huh!

AFTER-DINNER TOMMY

AS YOU KNOW, I'M NOT KNOWN AS A GREAT AFTER-DINNER SPEAKER. BEFORE DINNER, I'M MARVELLOUS! BUT AFTER DINNER, FORGET IT! I'M SORRY YOU DIDN'T KNOW THAT. BECAUSE, IF YOU'D ASKED ME TO SPEAK BEFORE DINNER, YOU WOULD HAVE HEARD A WONDERFUL SPEECH AND SAVED ALL THIS MONEY ON FOOD!

TO GIVE A SPEECH YOU HAVE TO HAVE A LOT OF CHARM, PERSONALITY, WIT – ANYWAY, I DON'T WANT TO TALK ABOUT MYSELF. I AM VERY PLEASED TO HAVE BEEN INVITED HERE THIS EVENING. THE ONLY THING I CAN SAY – IT COULDN'T HAVE HAPPENED TO A NICER MAN.

I'VE JUST HAD SOME WONDERFUL NEWS FROM MY DOCTOR AND HE SAID I'M LIVING – SO IF I DIE A DEATH IT'S FROM NOW ON!

WHAT A HECTIC LIFE IT IS IN SHOW BUSINESS – EVERY DAY I'M UP AT THE CRACK OF NOON!

LAST NIGHT I DREAMT MY WATCH WAS GONE. GOT RIGHT UP TO LOOK FOR IT AND I WAS LUCKY! IT WASN'T GONE, BUT IT WAS GOING. IT'S REALLY A WONDERFUL WATCH THOUGH. LAST WEEK I DROPPED IT ON THE FLOOR, BUT IT DIDN'T BREAK – IT FELL ON ITS HANDS.

MY SON DROVE ME HERE TODAY. HE'S BOUGHT A BRAND-NEW ELECTRIC CAR. IT'S MARVELLOUS. YOU CAN GET FROM LONDON TO MANCHESTER FOR ONLY FIVE POUNDS, BUT IT COSTS £20,000 FOR THE FLEX.

I DECIDED TO BECOME AN INVENTOR ONCE. FOR MY FIRST EXPERIMENT I CROSSED A MULE WITH A COW AND I GOT MILK WITH A KICK IN IT. THEN I CROSSED A PIG WITH AN ELEPHANT AND GOT THE BIGGEST PORK CHOPS IN TOWN. THEN I CROSSED KANGAROOS WITH RACOONS AND GOT FUR COATS WITH POCKETS.

MY NEXT-DOOR NEIGHBOUR IS ALWAYS MAKING THINGS LIKE AN INVENTOR – ONE DAY HE TOOK AN AXLE FROM A FORD AND A CHASSIS FROM A BENTLEY – HE GOT FIVE YEARS.

MY NEXT-DOOR NEIGHBOUR – THE SAME ONE – HE SAID TO ME, 'YOU'VE GOT TO GET RID OF THAT DOG.' I SAID, 'WHY?' HE SAID, 'HE KEEPS CHASING PEOPLE ON A BICYCLE.' I SAID, 'WELL, TAKE HIS BIKE AWAY.'

AND NOW LET ME LEAVE YOU WITH THESE FINAL WORDS – AS I SAID TO MY AGENT THE OTHER DAY, STOP WALKING ON TOP OF THE WATER WHILE I'M FISHING!

One of Tommy's favourite tricks. He said it always went down well at home. For an encore he would follow it with mash and gravy.

THE FLOATING SAUSAGE

You've seen the world's greatest magicians cause beautiful ladies to float through the air. This I can assure you is a lot less expensive and doesn't require an HGV to get your equipment to the theatre!

You don't even need to take a trip to the butcher's. All you need to do is hold the outstretched fingers of each hand horizontally in front of you, with their tips touching just a few inches in front of the bridge of your nose. Keep the other fingers bent back into the palms.

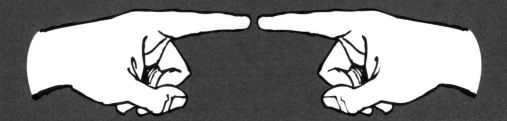

Now fix your gaze upon a point on the wall ahead in such a way that you can still see your fingers, even though they are out of focus. Then separate the fingertips slightly. You will see a sausage – or something remarkably like one – floating unaided between the two index fingers. Just make sure you do not focus on your fingers or the sausage will disappear, which is another trick entirely!

THE EGGS AND GLASSES

Now here we have four glass tumblers.
Un — deux — three — !

And one plastic tray.

(Tommy wobbles tray)

I don't know why I did that!

Now what I do is this. I fill this glass with water and that one there — there — and that one there.

(Tommy takes a sip from one of the glasses ...)

You know, it will never sell!

Now I put the plastic tray on there like that. Now the trick is this.

I have six fresh eggs. Now these eggs are so fresh the hens haven't missed them yet.

Now I'd like someone here at random —

oh, Mr Random — would you point at any egg you like, sir. This one? Why this one? Why not that one? What do you want to pick that one for? This one. All right.

Now what I'm going to do is this. I have four tubes. I put one tube there and another tube there like that — another one there — and the other one there. So that's four tubes on four glasses.

And I've got four fresh
eggs. Now I can't break
these, otherwise I'll
have no trick left. So
we assume they're all
right. I place one on
there — one there —
another there and the
last one on there. Now,

the trick is this — what I have to do — I've
got the water there to break the fall of the
eggs, see. And what I have to do — I shall go
like that see —

*(Tommy makes striking
movement with hand)*

or I may go like that —
I don't know — and the
idea of the trick is
this. I go like that
and the tray goes over
there and the eggs —
huh huh huh — they're supposed to go into the
glasses.

I want to know why it hasn't worked yet! I'd
also like to point out, sir, that you are in
direct line of fire!

I mean, if I got one egg in, it would still
be a good trick, wouldn't it?

Yes? It would, wouldn't it? And I'd like to
tell you — I'll give you a little tip — if the
eggs fly out — towards you — if they do — just
catch them like that —
not like that

(He claps his hands
together)

— else it will go all
over you!

Now what I want you to
do is this, count,
'One — two — three.'

That's what I want you to do...

Here we go now — the big trick — the one
you've all been waiting for — I want you all
to count — 'One — two — three.'

One — two — two and a
half...

(Tommy hits the tray
smartly with the heel
of his hand)

Thank you very much!

(If all goes to plan
the tray goes one way, the tubes another and
the four eggs arrive in the glasses below.)

That's four more than normal!

TRY IT YOURSELF

Fancy having a go at something like that yourself? Wait no longer. Here is an instant juggling act that requires little practice. It might even make you a star – or the maker of the messiest omelette there ever was!

Line up a table, a glass tumbler, a hard-boiled egg (once you have mastered the trick, you may use a raw one), the sleeve of a box of matches, a small shallow round baking tin, and a broom with stiff bristles – like those used by gardeners and witches! It is important that there is lots of spring in the bristles.

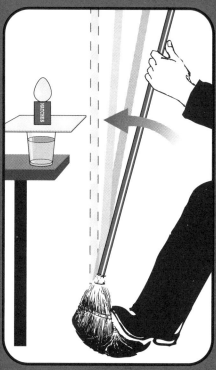

Fill the glass about two thirds with water. Place it near the edge of the table. Put the baking tin on top of the tumbler as shown. The tin should extend out about an inch or two over the table edge. On top of the tin, stand the matchbox sleeve with the egg – pointed end up – balanced in the open end of the box.

Stand the broom up so that it touches the edge of the tin as shown by the straight dotted line in the illustration. Then place your foot on the bristles and pull the broom handle back toward you and away from the edge of the table and the tin. Count to three, take a deep breath and let go of the handle.

The broom will spring back against the table and the tin with amazing results. The tin and the matchbox will be knocked smartly away and the egg should fall into the water – without breaking – with the most impressive plop. And if you don't get the egg in first time, keep at it until you get the knack. Just make sure you practise with a hard-boiled egg.

TOMMY'S ONE-LINERS

HERE'S A QUICK JOKE. I MUST TELL YOU THIS. I WANT TO HEAR IT MYSELF.

I'M GOING TO WORK VERY FAST TONIGHT. BEFORE YOU GET A CHANCE TO HATE ME I SHALL BE GONE.

THERE ARE ONLY TWO WAYS TO DO ANYTHING ... NOW AND LATER.

I DON'T HAVE TO DO THIS FOR A LIVING – I COULD ALWAYS LOSE WEIGHT AND BE A JOCKEY AGAIN.

I WENT TO BUY SOME CAMOUFLAGE TROUSERS THE OTHER DAY, BUT COULDN'T FIND ANY.

MY FRIEND DROWNED IN A BOWL OF MUESLI. HE WAS PULLED IN BY A STRONG CURRANT.

WHAT DO YOU GIVE A CANNIBAL WHO IS LATE FOR HIS DINNER? THE COLD SHOULDER.

WORK FASCINATES ME – I CAN SIT AROUND AND WATCH IT FOR HOURS.

I MISSED MY NAP THIS MORNING – I DID – SLEPT RIGHT THROUGH IT!

I NEVER MAKE MISTAKES – I THOUGHT I DID ONCE, BUT I WAS MISTAKEN.

Never Play Cards With Strangers

Just remember one thing – Lady Godiva put everything she had on a horse!

Offer the pack for shuffling. Take it back, fan the cards and have one chosen and noted. While the victim – sorry, spectator – shows his card to the others in the audience, you secretly remember the card at the bottom of the pack. This will be what is known as your key card. Have the chosen card replaced on top of the pack and the cards cut several times. The chosen card will now be lost somewhere in the pack.

You now announce that you will – surprise, surprise – attempt to find his chosen card. You deal the cards singly from the top of the face-down pack into a face-up pile. Keep dealing until you come to the key card. The next card dealt will be the selected one, the identity of which you must commit to memory. Then deal another four or five cards more. Take the next card and deal it face-down separately apart from the others. You now smugly bet the victim a drink that the next card you turn over will be his chosen card. He will have noticed that you missed his card four or five cards back and will gladly accept the bet. At this point you do not turn over the face-down card, but go back to the face-up cards, find the chosen one and turn that card over face-down.

Clever, eh!

IT'S IMPOSSIBLE!

I FEEL GOOD TONIGHT – I COULD CRUSH A GRAPE!

THE STUNTS THAT FOLLOW MIGHT SOUND AS IF THEY
ARE AS EASY AS CRUSHING A GRAPE OR SQUASHING A
TOMATO – UNTIL YOU TRY THEM!

ASK SOMEONE TO HOLD AN ORDINARY WOODEN SAFETY
MATCH BETWEEN THE FINGERS OF ONE HAND AS
SHOWN IN THE ILLUSTRATION. IT MUST LIE ACROSS
THE BACK OF THE MIDDLE FINGER – NEAR THE TIP
AND UNDER THE INDEX AND THIRD FINGERS. THE
CHALLENGE NOW IS TO KEEP THE FINGERS STRAIGHT
AND BREAK THE MATCH. HOWEVER HARD YOU PRESS UP
WITH THE MIDDLE FINGER OR DOWN WITH THE OTHER
TWO, IT CAN'T BE DONE – EVEN IF YOU ARE THE
STRONGEST MAN IN THE WORLD. TRY IT AND SEE.

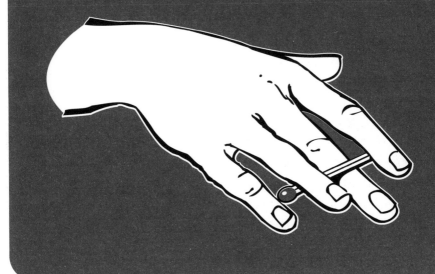

THIS FEAT – IN THE SAME CATEGORY – REQUIRES A LITTLE MORE PREPARATION. TIE A MEDIUM-SIZED BOOK TO THE MIDDLE OF A STRONG PIECE OF CORD OR STRING ABOUT FIVE FEET IN LENGTH. NOW, HOLDING ONE END OF THE CORD IN EACH HAND, YOU HAVE TO STRAIGHTEN OUT THE CORD ALONG AN ABSOLUTELY LEVEL PLANE. TO GET EXTRA TENSION AND INCREASE YOUR GRIP, YOU'RE ALLOWED TO WRAP THE CORD AROUND YOUR FISTS AS SHOWN. IT LOOKS EASY UNTIL YOU TRY, BUT YOU WILL NEVER SUCCEED IN STRETCH-ING OUT THE STRING IN SUCH A WAY THAT THERE IS NOT A KINK WHERE THE BOOK WEIGHS IT DOWN.

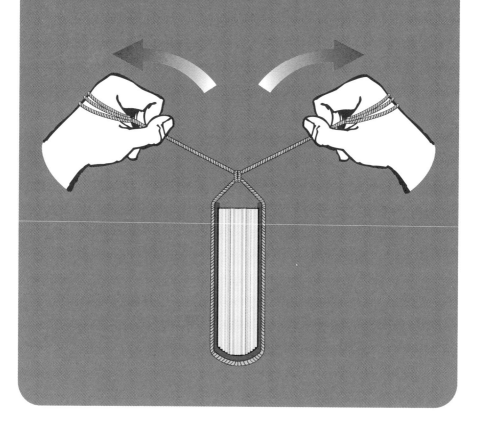

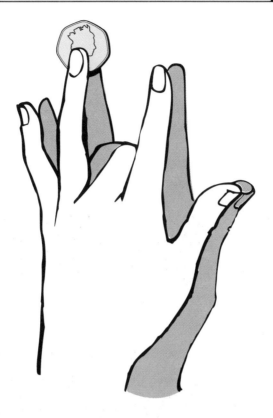

FOR THE THIRD OF THESE IMPOSSIBLE IMPOSSIBILITIES, PLACE YOUR HANDS TOGETHER SO THAT PALM IS TOUCHING PALM, FINGER TOUCHING FINGER, AND THUMB TOUCHING THUMB – BUT WITH THE SECOND FINGER OF EACH HAND BENT INWARD AND TUCKED OUT OF THE WAY ALONG THE SECOND JOINT FROM THE FINGERTIP. THE ILLUSTRATION SHOWS YOU HOW. NOW ASK A FRIEND TO SLIDE A COIN BETWEEN THE TIPS OF BOTH THIRD FINGERS. ALL YOU HAVE TO DO NOW IS DROP THE COIN – WITHOUT SEPARATING THE OTHER FINGERTIPS. TRY AS HARD AS YOU WILL, YOU WILL FIND YOUR FINGERS ARE INEXTRICABLY LOCKED TOGETHER.

IMPRESSIONS

AND NOW, LADIES AND GENTLEMEN, BY GOING BEHIND THIS CURTAIN FOR A BRIEF INSTANT AT A TIME I WOULD LIKE TO GIVE YOU IMPRESSIONS OF FAMOUS PEOPLE AND FAMOUS COUNTRIES IN THE WORLD ...

UNCLE SAM

JOHN BULL

I DON'T KNOW WHO THAT IS!

NAPOLEON

DON'T KEEP GIVING ME THAT!

ENGLISH SAILOR

AMERICAN SAILOR

TWO SAILORS AT ONCE

THE KING OF NORWAY

THE OTHER WAY!

YOU'RE DRIVING ME NUTS!

GET THOSE ELEPHANTS OFF THE STREET!

FROM THAT WONDERFUL FILM, THE *PRISONER OF ZENDA*

NELSON

HALF-NELSON

WE SHOULD NOT HAVE LOST THE WAR!

WHY?

AND FINALLY AN EXCERPT FROM THE DESERT SONG – DO YOU LIKE THE COAT?

IT'S GENUINE CAMEL HAIR. IT IS! LOOK AT THAT!

UP IN THE AIR

AND REMEMBER – IF AT FIRST YOU DON'T SUCCEED, THEN SKY-DIVING IS NOT FOR YOU!

You'll need five people to take part in this experiment in levitation, including the individual to be sent on a journey to the ceiling. It doesn't seem to make any difference how tall or large that person is. It should even work on someone with the gangling bulk of Tommy himself.

Request the subject to sit in a chair with his hands upon his lap. It is essential that he relaxes throughout. The other four must stand two on each side of the subject and place their closed fists together with forefingers extended as shown. One of the four must place his two extended forefingers beneath the subject's left armpit, another place his beneath the right armpit, a third beneath the left knee, and the last beneath the subject's right knee. It would appear that it would be absolutely impossible to lift someone as heavy as Tommy Cooper, seated as he is, with those fingers alone. It is important that whoever your subject is you try this first – as hard as you can. It is unlikely he will budge. Maybe he will topple over. Failure at this stage of the game is, in fact, important.

Once the subject has resettled in the chair, all four accomplices – without losing any time – place their hands one on top of the other on top of the subject's head and press down firmly. Count to ten as you apply a steady pressure. When you reach ten, all eight hands must be withdrawn immediately and repositioned in their original places. Without delay, repeat the lifting process with the extended forefingers. This time the subject will seem that much lighter and go soaring several feet into the air. The business of pressing down with the hands causes the subject to resist by exerting a vertical pressure in return and prepare him – mentally and physically – for the experience to follow.

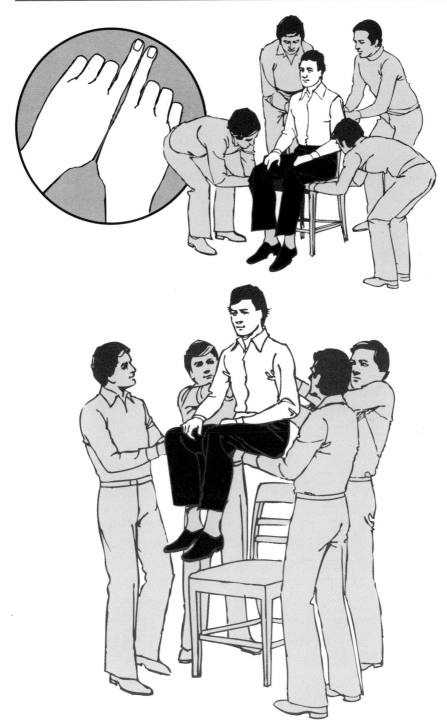

LAUGHTER MISCELLANY ONE

THERE'S A MAN RINGS UP A PUB ABOUT FOUR O'CLOCK IN THE MORNING AND HE SPEAKS TO THE OWNER AND THE OWNER SAYS, 'WHAT DO YOU MEAN RINGING ME UP AT FOUR O'CLOCK IN THE MORNING?' AND HE SAYS, 'WELL, WHAT TIME DO YOU OPEN?' HE SAYS, 'YOU CAN'T GET IN HERE UNTIL TWELVE O'CLOCK.' HE SAYS, 'I DON'T WANT TO GET IN. I WANT TO GET OUT!'

IT'S NOT GENUINELY KNOWN, BUT ONE OUT OF EVERY FIVE PEOPLE IS AN IDIOT. SO GET TOGETHER WITH FOUR FRIENDS – AND IF THEY'RE ALL RIGHT – IT'S YOU!

WHEN I WAS YOUNG MY PARENTS ENCOURAGED ME TO PUT ALL MY PENNIES IN A LITTLE METAL BOX. TO TEACH ME THRIFT, THEY SAID. I WAS TWENTY-ONE BEFORE I DISCOVERED THAT THE METAL BOX WAS THE GAS METER!

MY PEOPLE ARE IN THE IRON AND STEEL BUSINESS. MY MOTHER IRONS WHILE MY FATHER STEALS.

POLICE ARRESTED TWO KIDS YESTERDAY. ONE WAS DRINKING BATTERY ACID, THE OTHER WAS EATING FIREWORKS. THEY CHARGED ONE AND LET THE OTHER OFF.

A MAN CAME INTO MY DRESSING ROOM – SMILING HE WAS – AND HE SAID, 'YOU REMEMBER ME?' I SAID, 'YES. IT WAS THE EMPIRE, SUNDERLAND.' HE SAID, 'NO.' I SAID, 'THE PALACE, MANCHESTER? HE SAID, 'NO.' I SAID, 'THE HIPPODROME, BRISTOL?' HE SAID, 'NO – OF COURSE YOU REMEMBER ME – I'M YOUR BROTHER!'

THE RIDDLE SKETCH

Tommy's love of riddles and word play goes without saying to anyone familiar with his act. Here is a very early sketch worked by him in summer season and revue. The straight man would have been recruited from the supporting cast. The girl would have been the lead singer or – to use a word not heard in entertainment circles today – soubrette.

Straight man: It's not my sister and it's not my brother – still it's the son of my father and mother? Who is it?

Tommy: Well, who is it?

Straight man: I wouldn't know. I've never met your father or mother.

Tommy: No – it's a riddle.

Straight man: Your mother gave birth to a riddle?

Tommy: No. It's not my sister and it's not my brother – still it's the son of my father and mother. Who is it?

Straight man: I don't know.

Tommy: It's me!

Straight man: Oh, really! Congratulations.

Tommy: Do the riddle on our singing star.

Girl enters to applause

Tommy: You look like a million.

Girl: That's fantastic – I'm not a day over thirty!

Tommy: Go on – ask her.

Straight man: Oh yes – I have a riddle. How does it go?

Tommy: It's not my sister and it's not my brother – still it's the son of my father and mother. Who is it?

Riddle

It's not my sister it's not my brother
~ still it's the son of my father
Mother – who is it?

T. Well, who is it?

F. I wouldn't know, I've no...
...other Mother!

T:- No it's a riddle

F - Your Mother, gave...

F. or:- (Repeat...

F:- I don't know...

T. It's...

F. Oh, really - congratulations

T:- Do the riddle on — Name...
L & G. our singing star - (name)

T. You look like a million

G:- That's fantastic - I'm not a story any...

T. Go on, ask her.

F. ask her. - well I've only just met...

T. No, no! The riddle

F. Oh, yes there a riddle — well who is
How does it go.

T:- Repeats!

F. I've got it - It...

T. Try once more! Repeats!

F. I think I've got it! - It's not
my brother or my sister but a son
of my F & M. who is it?

G:- I think it's you

F. You silly girl _I It's him!!!

Straight man: I've got it. It wasn't my sister or my brother – and there was some doubt about my mother.

Tommy: Try once more. It's not my sister and it's not my brother – still it's the son of my father and mother. Who is it?

Straight man: I think I've got it. It's not my brother or my sister but a son of my father and mother. Who is it?

Girl: I think it's you.

Straight man: You silly girl. No – it's him!!!

RIDDLE-ME-REE

Here's a more magical approach to the subject of riddles.

- You'll need a pin. Concentrate on one of the riddles shown on the page opposite. Ideally it should be one to which you do not know the answer.

- Think of any number over ten and – let's say – under twenty.

- Hold the point of the pin on the dot opposite your chosen riddle.

- Count upward – with the tip of the pin – calling the first dot (the one opposite your riddle) 'one', the next 'two', and so on *in a circular anti-clockwise direction* until you come to your chosen number. Pause with the pin on this dot.

- Begin counting at 'one' again, starting on the dot at which you stopped, but this time *counting clockwise around the circle part of the question mark only.* Stop once you reach your selected number.

- Lift the page slightly and carefully press the pin through the dot on which you ended up after the second count.

- Having made the hole, take out the pin and hold your breath!

- Turn the page and find the pinprick. Check the number against it. Then refer to the corresponding words above.

They should solve the riddle of your choice – even though you had an absolutely free choice of number!

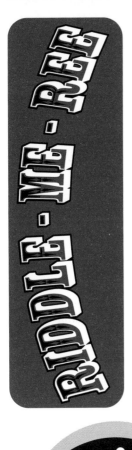

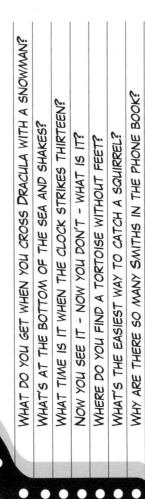

WHAT DO YOU GET WHEN YOU CROSS DRACULA WITH A SNOWMAN?

WHAT'S AT THE BOTTOM OF THE SEA AND SHAKES?

WHAT TIME IS IT WHEN THE CLOCK STRIKES THIRTEEN?

NOW YOU SEE IT – NOW YOU DON'T – WHAT IS IT?

WHERE DO YOU FIND A TORTOISE WITHOUT FEET?

WHAT'S THE EASIEST WAY TO CATCH A SQUIRREL?

WHY ARE THERE SO MANY SMITHS IN THE PHONE BOOK?

1 A BLACK CAT ON A ZEBRA CROSSING!

2 CLIMB A TREE AND ACT LIKE A NUT!

3 FROSTBITE!

4 THEY ALL HAVE PHONES!

5 A NERVOUS WRECK!

6 EXACTLY WHERE YOU LEFT HIM!

7 TIME TO GET IT REPAIRED!

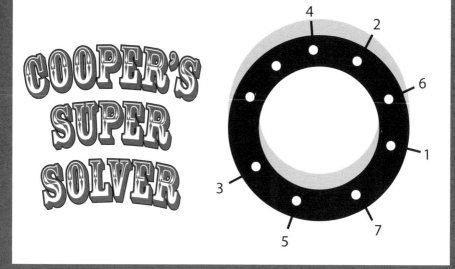

COOPER'S SUPER SOLVER

IN ALL DIRECTIONS

I SAID, 'DOCTOR, DOCTOR, I'VE LOST ALL SENSE OF DIRECTION. WHAT SHALL I DO?' HE SAID, 'GET LOST!'

Here's how to cadge a quick drink in the bar. Take a piece of card and draw a big bold arrow on it pointing to right or left. Prop it up against a bottle and bet the person next to you that he can't make the arrow point in the opposite direction without touching or turning the card in any way.

To claim your free drink, ask the barmaid for an empty glass and stand it in front of the card. Then take a jug of water and pour it into the glass until the water level exceeds the height of the arrow. The arrow changes direction before your very eyes – *just like that!*

Should you want to turn the arrow back in its original direction – just stand another glass in front of the first glass and pour away. And so on and so on …!

TOMMY'S LAUGHTER MEDICINE

I WOKE UP THIS MORNING WITH THIS TERRIBLE PAIN— SO I WENT TO THE DOCTOR. HE SAID, 'HAVE YOU HAD THIS PAIN BEFORE?' I SAID, 'YES.' HE SAID, 'WELL, YOU'VE GOT IT AGAIN!'

THIS CHAP RUSHED INTO THE SURGERY THE OTHER DAY WITH HIS ARM IN A SLING. THE DOCTOR SAID, 'HAVE YOU HURT YOUR ARM?' THE CHAP SAID, 'NO – I'VE HURT MY LEG.' THE DOCTOR SAID, 'WELL, IF YOU'VE HURT YOUR LEG, WHY HAVE YOU GOT YOUR ARM IN A SLING? HE SAID, 'I CAN'T GET MY LEG UP THAT HIGH!'

A FELLOW RUSHED INTO THE DOCTOR'S. HE SAID, 'DOCTOR, DOCTOR, I KEEP WANTING TO DRESS UP AS LADY HAMILTON!' THE DOCTOR SAID, 'WHAT DOES YOUR WIFE DO?' HE SAID, 'NOTHING – SHE JUST TURNS A BLIND EYE!'

THE DOCTOR GAVE HIM SIX MONTHS TO LIVE, BUT HE COULDN'T PAY HIS BILL, SO HE GAVE HIM ANOTHER SIX MONTHS!

WHEN YOU'RE IN HOSPITAL – WHY IS IT THEY ALWAYS KEEP PUTTING PILLOWS BEHIND YOU ALL THE TIME? HAVE YOU NOTICED THAT? THEY DO. A NURSE COMES IN AND PUTS A PILLOW BEHIND YOU AND ANOTHER PILLOW AND THEN ANOTHER ONE. YOU END UP SLEEPING STANDING UP!

WHEN I HAD MY HEART ATTACK, THEY GOT FIVE AMBULANCE MEN RACING ME TO HOSPITAL – I CAME IN THIRD! WHEN I CAME ROUND THE DOCTOR WAS SLAPPING MY WRISTS, WHICH ISN'T EASY WHEN YOUR HANDS ARE IN THE PRAYING POSITION!

COOPER'S CRAZY COMPASS

SEE THIS? IT'S ACTUALLY A COMPASS. I CAN'T TELL WHEN I'M LATE, BUT I KNOW WHERE I'M GOING.

If you want to confuse your sense of direction even further, this should do the trick.

Take a small square of cardboard – two and a half inches square is ideal – and cut off the corners to leave an octagon as in the illustration.

Draw an arrow on one side pointing north-west as shown. Then, holding the compass as in the third diagram between your left forefinger and thumb at its north and south points, swivel the card around. On the other side draw a second arrow, pointing in the same direction – to the north-west. Pivot the card around several times to make sure.

'You will see that both arrows point in the same direction.'

Now, this is where things get confusing. Change your hold on the card so that the arrow points towards the tip of your forefinger as in the fourth diagram. Now when you pivot the card around you will find that the two arrows are at complete cross purposes. Instead of pointing in the same direction, they now point at right angles to each other.

'Now they're at a crossroads – they don't seem to know which way they want to go.'

Then shift your hold again so that the arrow points as in the final diagram. When you pivot the card now, the arrows will point in opposite directions.

'You could say this is the ideal compass for people who don't know whether they're coming or going!'

The whole trick depends upon getting the arrows drawn exactly as described and also the careful handling of the compass between the appropriate corners.

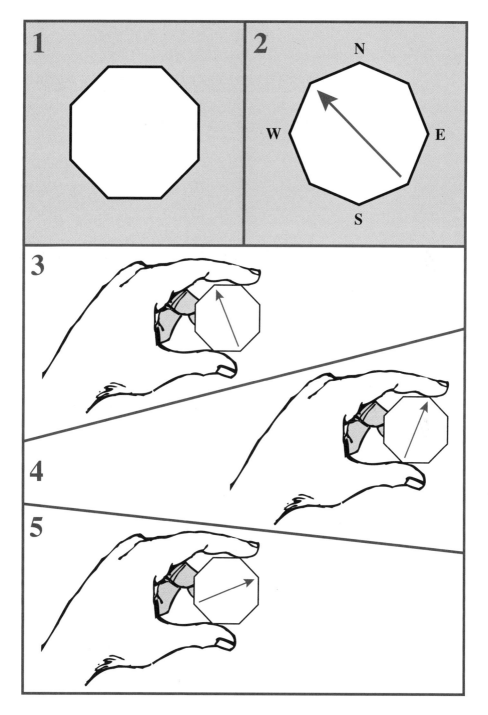

UP THE GARDEN PATH

This is the easiest thing in the book – but tread carefully!

In the illustration you will see ten numbers of varying sizes. Read them out to a friend quite quickly, beginning at the bottom of the path with seventy-seven and travelling all the way to the top. As you call out each number, all your friend has to do is call out loud the number next in sequence. When you say 'seventy-seven', they say 'seventy-eight', and so on. If you like, you can have someone write down the replies on a sheet of paper.

Once you've climbed the path, turn the page. Here are the numbers.

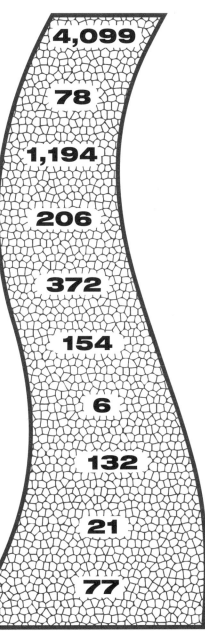

Everyone who has a go at this is sure it's as easy as pie. In fact, most people fail spectacularly on the final number. They call out 'five thousand,' when what they should say, of course, is 'four thousand, one hundred!'

When they're recovering from the shock of the above, challenge someone that they can't count from ten to one backwards without making a mess of the whole thing.

Slowly and smugly most people will count, '10, 9, 8, 7, 6, 5, 4, 3, 2, 1' and then heave a sigh of relief. But if you make this the subject of a bet, people are bound to lose. Remind the victim that – literally speaking – to count backwards from ten to one goes, '1, 2, 3, 4, 5, 6, 7, 8, 9, 10!'

WHY WAS SIX SCARED OF SEVEN?
BECAUSE SEVEN ATE NINE.

HOLIDAY TIME

I went to Majorca for my holidays. We went by Jumbo Jet – the pilot was an elephant! And when we got to the hotel, they gave us the red-carpet treatment. They did. I thought that's very nice of them. Then they said, 'The beds are not ready – so you've got to sleep on the red carpet!'

And I got up to the room and there was no ceiling to the room. So I rang the manager and told him, 'There's no ceiling to my room.' He said, 'That's all right. The man above doesn't walk around much.'

When it came to lunchtime, we asked the manager, 'Can we have a little wine with our meal?' He said, 'Yes,' and locked the dog out!

But the beach! The beach was something else. It wasn't sand, it was something else. But my wife doesn't like swimming. The last time she went near the water, the tide went out and refused to come back.

And when we got back from the holiday, I parked the car in the drive, took the luggage out of the back seat and helped the wife down from the roof rack. And there were 2,000 milk bottles on the doorstep. And I said to the milkman, 'I've been away on my holiday.' He said, 'Thank goodness for that. I was beginning to think you didn't like the stuff!'

And there was water everywhere, because my wife – she always leaves the tap running when we go away, because she's got a theory that it drowns burglars! And the cellar was about seven feet high in water. Seven feet. I was so surprised; I nearly fell off her shoulders. And it started to rise – the first floor, the second floor, the third floor – which I didn't understand. We live in a bungalow!

TOPSY-TURVY TUMBLERS

YOU CAN REPEAT THIS TRICK OVER AND OVER AGAIN UNTIL YOU DRIVE YOUR AUDIENCE TO DRINK!

This is the ideal stunt to drive a friend crazy. You line up three tumblers in a row, designating the one on the far left number one, the one in the middle number two, and the one at the far right number three. The glass in the middle should be right way up, the other two upside down. You then demonstrate how with three moves you can leave all three tumblers mouth upwards, ready for filling. Each move consists of turning over two tumblers at the same time, one tumbler in each hand.

You show how easy it is by turning

• Tumblers 2 and 3   • Tumblers 1 and 3   • Tumblers 2 and 3

calling out the positions as you do so. You must emphasise the numerical sequence: 'Two and three, one and three, two and three.'

Now challenge your victim to do the same, at which point you make the one sneaky move on which the whole deception is based. Nonchalantly turn the centre tumbler upside down. Nothing could seem fairer. Everyone will assume that the tumblers are back as they started, but there is a subtle difference. While the centre tumbler is still standing the opposite way to the two end tumblers, it is now mouth downwards while the other two are mouth upwards. However strictly he adheres to the 'two and three, one and three, two and three' moves, the tumblers will now end up all upside down.

It is the easiest thing now for you to show them again how it should be done. Simply turn over the middle glass and repeat the moves to take you back where you started – all mouth upwards. And so on ad infinitum.

HOW TO MAKE A HANDKERCHIEF DANCE

I WAS A DANCER ONCE. I DID SWAN LAKE. I FELL IN!

It sounds crazy and totally pointless, but it is possible for an ordinary white gentleman's handkerchief to be made to pirouette with the best of the ballet world.

Find as large a handkerchief as you possibly can and tie a single knot along the centre of one edge as shown in figure 2.

Then take hold of the two opposite lower corners and twirl the handkerchief over and over again, twisting it as tightly as possible. The more twists at this stage, the more spectacular the dance will be later. The handkerchief should end up looking something like figure 4.

Now double the twisted portion of the handkerchief over on to itself. Hold the two ends of this portion together in the right hand and the knotted portion in the left. The idea is that the knot represents the head, the twisted ends the legs.

Now if you let go of one of the legs and pull on the other one, the dancer will spin happily round on one foot while giving a perfect high kick with the other. Change your hold to the other leg and pull again – around she goes once more!

The stunt originated in America, where it is traditional to recite the following once the figure is formed:

FATIMA WAS A DANCER GAY.
FOR FIFTY CENTS SHE'D DANCE THIS WAY.

Here you move the legs backwards and forwards with a swaying motion.

BUT IF ONE DOLLAR YOU WOULD PAY,
SHE'D GO TA-RA-RA-BOOM-DE-AY.

On the last line, release the leg and the applause should be spontaneous.

Remember, it is important to put as many twists as you possibly can into the handkerchief at the beginning.

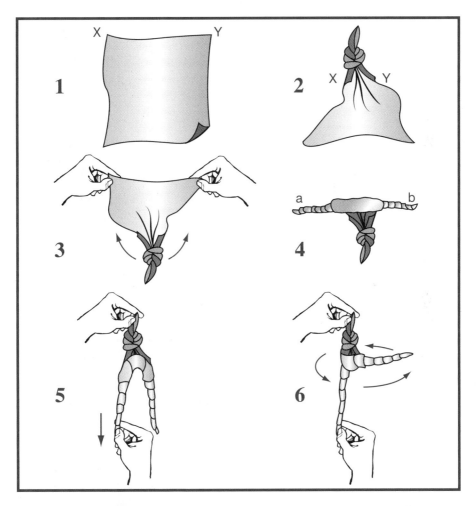

I'VE TIPTOED INTO THE HOUSE SO OFTEN AT FOUR O'CLOCK IN THE MORNING, THE NEIGHBOURS THINK I'M A BALLET DANCER.

THE UNPOPPABLE BALLOON

IF I CAN JUST GET RID OF THAT BANG ...!

'And now, ladies and gentlemen, I'd like to present for you the vanishing balloon trick – the trouble is I haven't got it quite right yet. There's one thing that bothers me and when I can get over that, it will be the greatest vanishing trick in the world.' *(Tommy takes a pin to the balloon, which bursts)* **'That's the thing that bothers me – if I can just get rid of that BANG …!'**

If you follow these instructions carefully, here's one way at least of getting rid of the bang when you stick a pin in a balloon.

In addition to the balloon and some pins or needles, you'll need scissors and a roll of clear Sellotape or similar adhesive tape. Inflate the balloon to a reasonable size – not too big – and tie a tight knot in the end. Then take a piece of Sellotape – about an inch square – and stick it to the balloon. Make sure that it does not wrinkle by smoothing it down gently. If you stick a pin through the centre of the Sellotape and the layer of the balloon attached to it, the balloon will not pop. Even at a short distance the Sellotape can hardly be seen on the surface of the balloon, although it will be even more invisible against a balloon with a pattern of some kind on its surface.

'BY ROYAL APPOINTMENT' -THE VANISHING STAMP

I JUST SPENT FIVE POUNDS ON STAMPS. IT'S NO GOOD.
I MUST FIND A CHEAPER POST OFFICE.

Even if you can't make a balloon vanish without its bang, here's a simple disappearing trick with which you can have fun at a bar. You can even start with the wild claim that you can make the Queen disappear. What you really mean is the head of the Queen as it appears on a postage stamp!

Place the stamp on the bar. Then ask for a clear glass tumbler. Position the glass on the stamp so that the stamp is completely covered and then pour water into the glass until it is about two-thirds full. Then take a saucer and place it over the glass. Whichever way you look, the stamp will be completely invisible.

Provided that no edge of the stamp protrudes from under the tumbler and that there is sufficient water in the glass, there is no way the stamp can be seen – all down to refraction of the light rays and related phenomena. Don't pass this one by because it is so easy. It is spectacularly effective for a stunt so simple.

TOMMY'S MAD TEA PARTY

PUT THE KETTLE ON ... IT SUITS YOU!

Talk about perfect casting – Tommy once played the part of the Mad Hatter in an audio recording of Lewis Carroll's *Alice's Adventures in Wonderland*. Sadly no one ever carried the idea through to one of the several film versions that were released during his career. It is hard to imagine a tea party with Tommy in charge without the man in the fez adding fun – like the following – to the festivities.

Start with three teacups and twelve lumps of sugar. You now have to divide the twelve lumps among the three cups in such a way that there is an odd number of lumps in each cup. Don't even begin to think of dissolving all the lumps in the tea and then distributing that between the three cups!

To achieve the sugar challenge, you have to cheat a little. Put five lumps in one cup and four in another. Then put the remaining three lumps into the third cup and place this cup so that it rests inside the second. One cup now has five lumps, another three, and the third seven lumps all told!

There is another way. This time place one lump in the first cup, another lump in the second cup, and then the remaining ten lumps in the third cup. Once again you have an odd number of lumps in each cup. As the Mad Hatter would have pointed out, ten is an extremely odd number of lumps to put into one cup of tea!

For the next stunt you will need just two teacups. The challenge is to lift the two cups without using your hands and to leave them both suspended in mid-air. We can assume that at a Cooper tea party balloons would be at hand. Simply take a balloon and arrange the cups and balloon as shown. Blow up the balloon and the pressure of the air will force the sides of the balloon into the cups. If you keep blowing, there will be enough pressure to push the surfaces of the rubber so far against the insides of the cups that you can lift the balloon with the teacups literally suspended in mid-air.

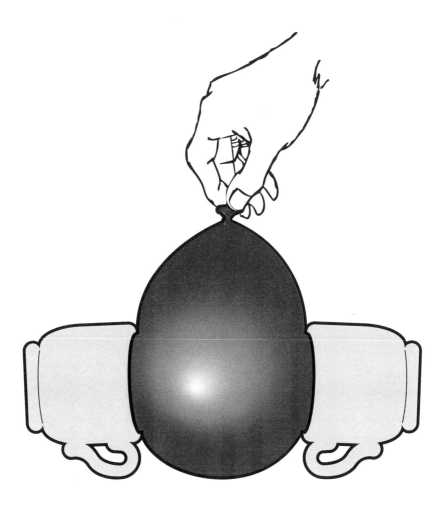

Finally, here is an impromptu favourite of many magicians, Tommy included. You need a single lump of sugar and a pencil. Ask somebody to name a letter of the alphabet and write the letter boldly on one side of the cube. Drop the sugar into a cup of tea and then guide their hand to rest over the top of the cup. Say Tommy's favourite magic words – *'Hocus Pocus, Fish Bones Choke Us'* – and assorted mumbo-jumbo, and then tell the helper to look at his or her palm.

To their amazement, they will see the chosen letter reproduced on their own hand.

Make sure that the pencil is of the soft variety and that when you write the letter on the sugar you do so as heavily as you can. Prior to dropping the cube in the cup of tea, take it between the forefinger and thumb of your left hand, with your thumb against the pencilled letter. If you press heavily, this will leave a reversed impression of the letter on your thumb. It helps if you are able to moisten the thumb secretly beforehand. Drop the sugar in the tea and as you guide the spectator's hand into position, transfer the impression from your thumb to their palm. It sounds obvious, but the trick is really startling, especially if you delay the revelation so that they have less opportunity to think back to reconstruct what has happened. Obviously, guiding their hand onto the cup should be done as casually as possible.

'GOING-UP- LADIES UNDERWEAR'

> I MET A FUNNY WOMAN LAST NIGHT!

WHAT'S THE GOOD OF HAVING A LIVING BRA WHEN YOU'VE GOT A FLAT CHEST?

You'll need a good-sized handkerchief or even better – because sturdier – a table napkin. There then follows what is best described as an exercise in cloth origami.

- First lay the napkin flat on the table and fold the right and left edges to meet in the centre as in the first illustration.

- Lift the napkin at the sides at the points marked X and Y so that it folds back on itself and place it down flat as shown.

- It is very important that you are clear about which corner is which. They are designated A, B, C and D.

- Take corners A and D with your left hand and corners B and C with your right hand. Avoid contact with any other part of the napkin.

- Lift the napkin between your hands and separate your hands as you do so, bringing the napkin against you chest.

- Hey presto – a lady's brassiere!

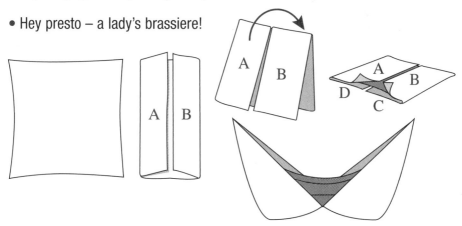

This trick was a big favourite of one of Tommy's early contemporaries – one of the most successful comedy magicians in America. It just so happens that she was a lady. Her name was Dell O'Dell.

COOPER'S PROPELLER

I ONCE WORKED IN A TOY FACTORY. I SOLD THOUSANDS OF TOPS. THEY WERE REAL MONEY SPINNERS.

Here's an impressive demonstration of juggling that is easier than it seems. All you need is a single cigarette paper.

 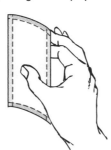 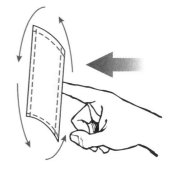

Fold it back on its original centre crease so that it will lie flat against the table. Now fold each of the four edges inwards about one eighth of an inch. These folds are then opened out almost flat so that you have what resembles a tiny tray. The folds are to make the paper more rigid than it apparently is.

Make sure your fingertips are thoroughly dry – moisture will not help what should follow – and then hold the paper lightly between the right forefinger and thumb at the exact centre as shown in the illustration. The forefinger should be against the back of the paper, the thumb against the concave side upon which the edges are folded upwards.

Now move the hand forward with a steady motion in a horizontal plane. As you do so, quickly remove the thumb and straighten out the forefinger so that it is pointing forward. As long as you keep this finger moving in a forward direction, the cigarette paper will go spinning round at the fingertip at a fairly high speed, defying gravity all the while. You can even keep the paper spinning as you walk along with your finger outstretched and, with a bit of practice, you can even loop the loop! Remember not to release the thumb until the hand is in motion. The folded edges of the paper catch the current of the air made by the movement of your hand and then science takes over.

GHOULISH TOMMY

DID YOU HEAR OF THE VAMPIRE WHO WANTED TO BECOME A VEGETARIAN? HE DIDN'T GET ANYWHERE BECAUSE HE COULDN'T GET BLOOD OUT OF A TURNIP!

Here are three simple tricks and gags that are perfect for Halloween or any occasion when you want to make somebody's hair stand on end.

The amputated thumb is not as grisly as it sounds. You require a small turnip that has become soft through being left out of the fridge for a few days. If you haven't got a turnip, a carrot will do. Cut it in such a way that it corresponds to your left thumb and conceal it in the folds of a paper napkin. Close your left hand into a fist with the thumb sticking up and cover it with the napkin. In the process get your thumb out of the way and grip the bottom end of the vegetable where the thumb was. Shape the napkin accordingly and ask a spectator to hold the thumb through the paper. The turnip or carrot will feel just like a thumb! Then cut though the vegetable with a sharp pair of scissors and be ready to revive one shocked spectator any way you can.

The dead finger illusion is creepy in a more subtle way. Simply grasp someone's left hand with your right hand with your two forefingers extended as in the illustration. Now ask the spectator to feel these two forefingers by running the forefinger and thumb of their free hand back and forth along them, the thumb touching their finger and the forefinger yours. This produces a strange sensation of numbness, as if their forefinger has lost some of its feeling.

This is a more graphic demonstration of the same theme. You'll need a small box with a lid. Something the size of a large matchbox – the type used for holding those big household matches – is ideal. Make a hole at one end of the bottom of the box. It should be large enough for a finger to go through. Then pad the box with cotton wool, leaving a gap at the hole. The cotton wool, being fluffy, will mask the edges of the hole. Apply red colouring around this part – tomato ketchup, nail polish, whatever – and when you feel most prone to shock people, produce the box with the finger – your finger, of course – inside. Take off the lid and keep the finger still at first. Then watch them scream when you cause it to wriggle! A touch of powder applied to the finger to make it look dead will enhance the effect.

I GOT TO THINKING THE OTHER DAY - ISN'T IT FUNNY ALL THE GREAT STAGE MAGICIANS ARE DEAD HOUDINI'S DEAD. DANTE'S DEAD. JASPER MASKELYNE'S DEAD. COME TO THINK OF IT, I'M NOT FEELING SO WELL MYSELF.

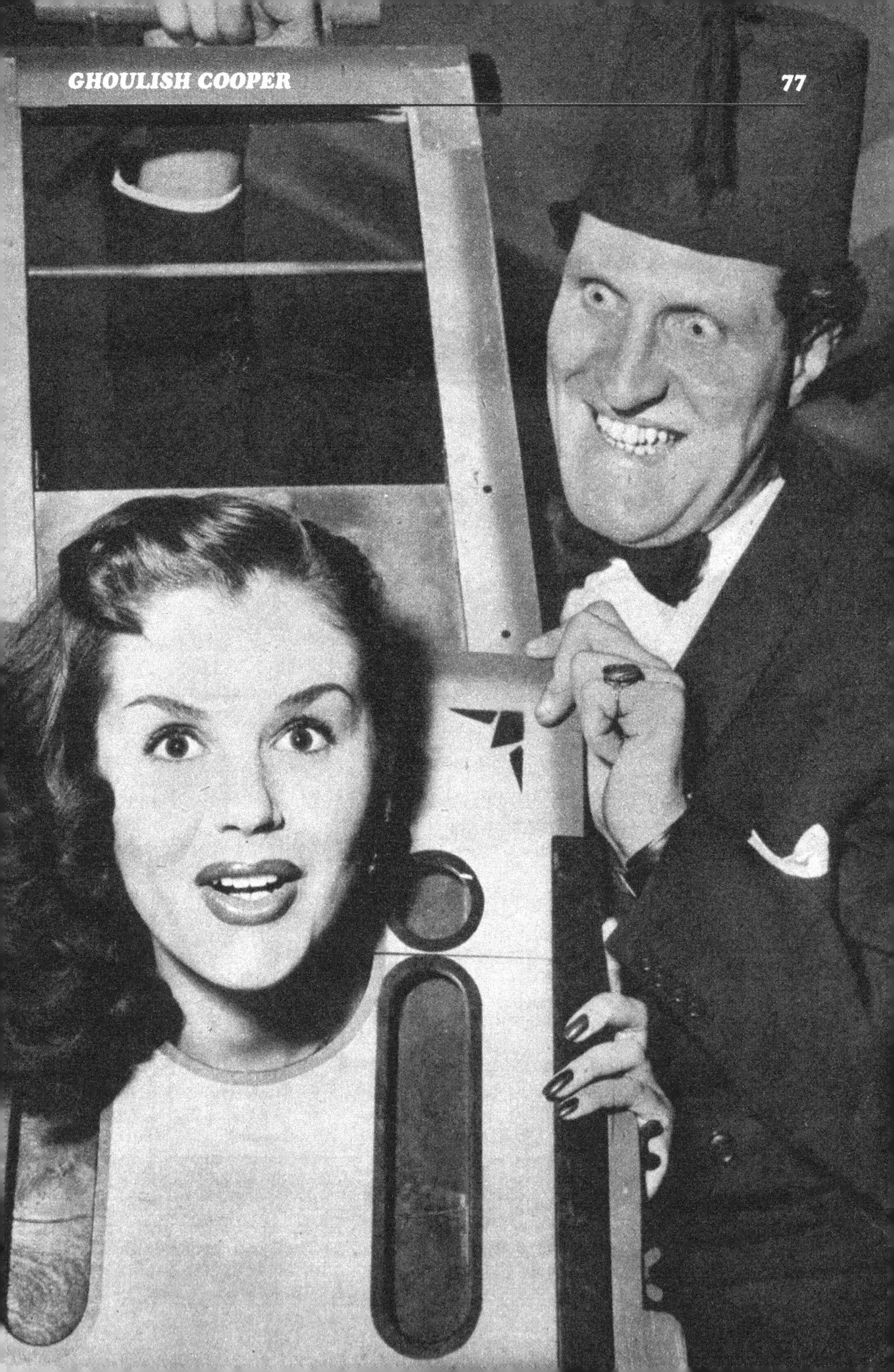

MEET THE WIFE

MY WIFE IS CRAZY ABOUT FURS AND SHE WANTED SOMETHING DIFFERENT. SO SHE WENT TO A FURRIER WHO DOES HIS OWN BREEDING. HE CROSSED A MINK WITH A GORILLA. SHE GOT A BEAUTIFUL COAT, ONLY THE SLEEVES ARE TOO LONG.

I DON'T KNOW WHAT TO GET HER FOR HER BIRTHDAY ANYMORE. FIRST SHE WANTED A MINK - SO I GOT HER A MINK. THEN SHE WANTED A SILVER FOX - SO I GOT HER A SILVER FOX. ISN'T IT SILLY? THE HOUSE IS FULL OF ANIMALS.

SHE GOT A TICKET FOR SPEEDING THE OTHER DAY. THE FUNNY PART WAS SHE WAS CHANGING A TYRE AT THE TIME.

I HAD A VERY TIRING JOURNEY UP TO BLACKPOOL THE OTHER DAY. IT WAS SO HOT. THERE WERE TWELVE PEOPLE IN THE CARRIAGE. THE WIFE HAD TO STAND ALL THE WAY.

AND THE OTHER NIGHT I TOOK HER TO A DANCE AND SHE WAS THE PRETTIEST GIRL ON THE FLOOR. I CAN STILL SEE HER LYING THERE!

SHE RAN OFF WITH THE MILKMAN ONCE. TEN MINUTES LATER SHE WAS BACK. I SAID, 'I THOUGHT YOU'D RUN OFF WITH THE MILKMAN?' SHE SAID, 'I DID, BUT HE RAN FASTER.'

SHE WATCHES SO MANY MYSTERY THRILLERS ON TELEVISION THAT WHEN SHE SWITCHES THE SET OFF, SHE WIPES HER FINGERPRINTS OFF THE DIAL!

SHE HAS SOME FUNNY HAIRSTYLES. LAST WEEK SHE HAD IT SHAPED LIKE A HAND. I SAID, 'WHAT'S THAT?' SHE SAID, 'A PERMANENT WAVE!'

VICTORIAN COOPER
- HOW TO WALK
THROUGH A POSTCARD

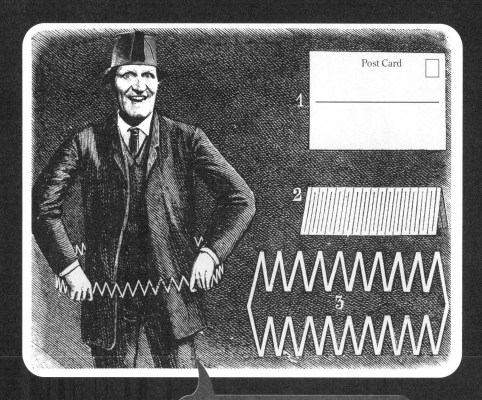

FANCY A FULLY GROWN MAN
DOING THIS!

This stunt goes back to Victorian times when scarcely a book about pastimes and what were quaintly called parlour amusements didn't include it in its pages. It is still surprising today, if you haven't come across it before.

It seems an out-and-out impossibility, but it is possible to cut a postcard in such a way that it will expand into a loop that you can pass over your head and step right through – if you are not too large.

With a straight edge and a sharp blade make a cut lengthwise down the centre of the postcard leaving about one sixteenth of an inch uncut at either end. Now very carefully fold the card in half lengthwise taking care not to tear the ends. Next, with the knife or a pair of very sharp scissors make a series of sideways slits as shown in the illustration, alternating from the edges of the card to the long centre slit and from the slit to the edges, each cut stopping short about one sixteenth of an inch from the long slit or the edges. Then very gently open up the card. You will be impressed as it expands into a very delicate ring of quite amazing size. Of course, the steadier your hand and the more sideways cuts you can accommodate, the larger the hole will be when you tease the thin strands of the postcard apart so that you can step through.

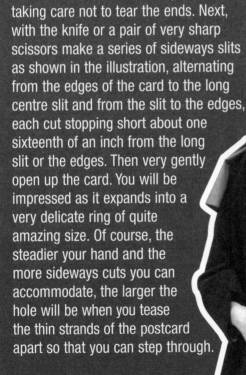

TIPSY TOMMY

> I'VE JUST JOINED ALCOHOLICS ANONYMOUS.
> I STILL DRINK, BUT NOW I USE A DIFFERENT NAME.

This is an almighty challenge. Offer to pay for the next round if anyone can balance the cork from a bottle of wine edge to edge on the rim of the bottle and then using only one hand pour the wine from the same bottle without disturbing the balance of the cork. Obviously if they can't – and you can – they must pay the tab.

The picture of Tommy tells all. You need a couple of forks. Stick them into the cork as shown, the prongs almost interlocking. The handles should point downwards. Because the cork's centre of gravity is shifted down-wards below the point of balance, the cork should balance quite easily on the rim of the bottle. While pouring directly from the bottle will alter the angle of the bottle itself, it will not disturb the cork which should remain upright provided you pour from the side of the rim opposite to the point of balance. You will not be able to empty the bottle, but you should be able to pour at least half the contents successfully – and certainly enough to win your bet. Obviously practise this a few times in private before going out to impress the big wide world.

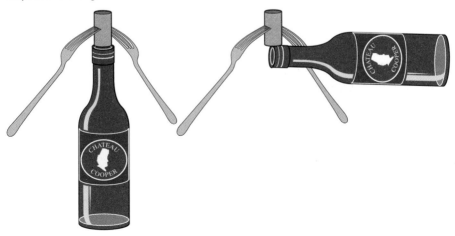

DROP EVERYTHING!

If you had fun emulating Tommy's antics with the corks and the bottle, you'll enjoy these similarly crazy combinations all devised to play games with gravity.

Start off with three drinking straws. Tape them together at one end and impale a grape or a cherry on the ends of the two outer straws. Then snip a short length off the free end of the centre straw. Take a fourth straw and balance the shorter straw as shown in the illustration. It is easier than it appears.

The configuration with the two forks, the coin and the needle stuck in the top of the candle is self-explanatory. What is not so obvious from the diagram, however, is that if you take extreme care it is possible to spin the coin around on the point of the needle.

Finally head for the stationery drawer and find a pencil, a ruler and a penknife. Open the knife halfway and stab the pencil as shown. No matter how sharp the pencil, it should stand to attention on the end of the ruler every time.

'WHERE DID THE DUCKS GO?'

I SHALL NOW PRODUCE FROM THIS EMPTY CLOTH FOUR LIVE DUCKS ...

THEY'VE GOT AWAY AGAIN!

LAUGHTER MISCELLANY TWO

I WAS IN MADAME TUSSAUD'S THE OTHER DAY AND THERE WAS A COUPLE THERE - JUST STANDING AND LOOKING, AS MOST PEOPLE DO. AND THE COMMISSIONAIRE WENT UP TO THEM AND SAID, 'LOOK, WILL YOU PLEASE KEEP MOVING. WE'RE STOCKTAKING!'

WHEN I WAS A KID I WAS BIG FOR MY SIZE - WELL OVER SIX FEET AND I WEIGHED FIFTEEN STONE. MY AMBITION WAS TO BE TWO JOCKEYS! AND AT CHRISTMAS MY FATHER USED TO SEND ME SKATING ON THE LAKE. I DON'T KNOW WHY. IT WASN'T FROZEN OVER.

THESE TWO FELLOWS MET. ONE SAID, 'DID YOU HEAR THAT SAM DIED?' THE OTHER SAID, 'DID HE LEAVE ANYTHING?' HE SAID, 'YES - EVERYTHING!'

THIS CANNIBAL INVITED HIS FRIEND HOME FOR DINNER. HIS FRIEND SAID, 'WHAT'S THAT I CAN SMELL?' THE CANNIBAL SAID, 'OH, THAT'S THE WIFE COOKING IN THE KITCHEN. SHE'LL BE DONE IN A MINUTE!'

THERE WAS THIS LITTLE BOY OF THREE. HIS UNCLES ALWAYS USED TO PAT HIM ON THE HEAD AND GIVE HIM SIXPENCE. NOW THAT KID IS A MILLIONAIRE - BUT HE'S GOT A FLAT HEAD.

SO I WENT TO THE DENTIST THE OTHER DAY. HE SAID, 'SAY, "AAAH!"' I SAID, 'WHY?' HE SAID, 'BECAUSE MY DOG'S DIED.'

'BETCHA CAN'T'

ANYONE CAN BE THE LIFE AND SOUL OF THE PARTY ONCE THEY CAN PERFORM A FEW BAFFLING TRICKS LIKE THE TRICKS I PERFORM IN MY ACT. THEY EVEN BAFFLE ME!

Here we are back in the free drinks department. Any one of these should deliver the goods accordingly, so take your pick.

You bet the first unsuspecting 'sucker' a round of drinks that he can't:

- Lift a fizzy drink bottle with a drinking straw without tying the straw around the bottle.

- Cut a length of string to which a cup is tied without the cup falling and without touching either the string or the cup after the cut has been made.

- Balance a glass on top of a banknote suspended flat across two other glasses.

- Remove an ice cube from a glass of water with a short length of string without tying any knots.

Turn the page to find out how to score every time.

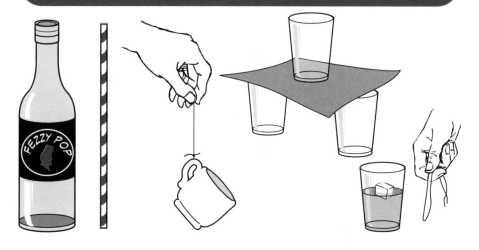

Put a sharp bend in the straw about one third from one end. Once inside the bottle, the end of the straw will spring out, hooking itself under the shoulder of the bottle. It is easy now to lift the bottle by the other end of the straw.

Tie a length of string to the handle of a cup and challenge someone to cut the string and leave the cup suspended as you dangle it before them. If they risk cutting without knowing the solution, the cup will fall to the ground, so beware of breakages. All you do to win the bet is tie a loop tightly in the string and cut the string through the loop.

Place two identical glasses – small shot glasses work best – a few inches apart so that a banknote rests comfortably on top as a bridge between the two. Obviously a third glass placed in the centre of the note will cause it to collapse. However, if you pleat the note lengthwise with accordion-style folds, it becomes surprisingly rigid and will withstand the weight of the glass.

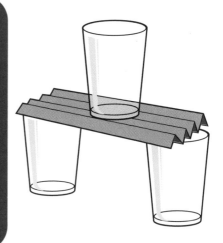

When people have given up trying to lasso the ice cube, take the string – or a length of thread may work more easily – soak it in the water and then double it into a loop at the centre. Rest the loop on the top of the ice cube and pour salt over both. After a while you will be able to lift the ice cube with the string, which will have become frozen to it. What happens is that the salt causes the ice to melt. Stop pouring the salt and the water that results on top of the ice cube will refreeze, this time around the string.

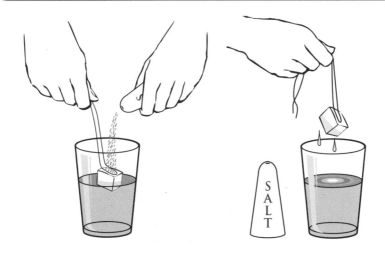

INTO THIN AIR
-THE FLYAWAY COIN

> WITH THIS LARGE
> HANDKERCHIEF I CAN
> VANISH AN ELEPHANT.
> THERE'S ONLY ONE SNAG -
> THE HANDKERCHIEF CAN'T
> BE EXAMINED!

Here's a simple way to duplicate the skills of the great masters of sleight-of-hand. Tommy Cooper himself was, of course, far more adept at actual legerdemain than his public image revealed, although he would not have been averse to using a method like the one that follows to make a coin disappear.

Secretly get an elastic band around the fingertips and thumb of your left hand. Cover the hand with a handkerchief as shown in the illustration. Borrow a coin and place it in the centre of the cloth, with the left fingers and the handkerchief closing around the coin. This will enable the elastic band, which must be a snug fit, to trap the coin accordingly. All you have to do now is pronounce the magic word and grab the handkerchief with the right hand by one of the corners. Let go with the left hand and shake the handkerchief out dramatically. To all intents and purposes the coin has disappeared. The owner of the coin will probably be more concerned about the return of his money than inspecting the handkerchief. Besides, in the words of Tommy's friend, the American comedy magician, Jay Marshall, 'If you wipe your nose on the handkerchief before you put it in your pocket, very few spectators will ask to examine it!'

BILLCATCHER

My father once said to me, 'It doesn't matter if you let love slip through your fingers or even money slip through your fingers, but if you let your fingers slip through your fingers, you're in trouble.' That's semi-jolly, isn't it?

You take the bill in the restaurant and explain to your lunch partner that when you drop it, he has to catch it before it hits the floor. If he succeeds, you'll pick up the tab. If he fails, he must do the honours. You demonstrate on yourself and everything seems straightforward. But when he goes to grab the bill, he gets nowhere.

The secret is all a matter of fingers and thumbs and the natural delay in reaction reflexes. You must hold the bill between your finger and thumb at one end, the length of the bill pointing downwards. The other fellow must position his own finger and thumb on either side of the bill at the centre – as close as he can get to the paper without making contact. You would think this would give him an advantage.

Explain that he has to catch the bill when you drop it, but that he mustn't do anything until you do so. When you do let go, it will slip right through his fingers before he has had a chance to register his senses. Just make sure that there are no bends or creases in the bill and that when you release the paper, you do so suddenly – as a surprise – without giving any advance warning.

The reason you can catch the bill when you demonstrate it on yourself, is because your own brain is in possession of all the facts needed to synchronise your actions. Needless to say, the stunt works equally well with a crisp, uncrumpled banknote. The words choose themselves: 'If you can catch it, you can keep it!'

TEARAWAY TOMMY

NOW I WANT YOU TO TAKE A CARD - ANY CARD. NOW TEAR IT INTO HALVES - TEAR IT INTO QUARTERS - TEAR IT INTO EIGHTHS - AND THROW THE PIECES UP IN THE AIR. INSTANT CONFETTI! HAPPY NEW YEAR!

Take a strip of paper – half a sheet of A4 cut lengthwise is ideal – and make two tears or cuts in it as shown in the picture. You now challenge a friend to hold one end in each hand and to tear the strip into three pieces. It appears easy enough, especially since the original tears are obviously the same length, but when he or she – or even for that matter you – pulls the paper apart only one side is torn straight through. Unless, of course, you hold the centre marked X in your teeth – but that's cheating! It doesn't matter how close the two original tears or cuts go to the opposite edge of the strip – only one end will be torn free.

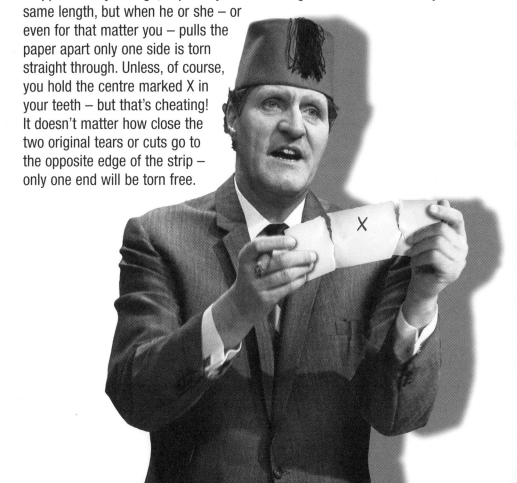

COMEDY LEVITATION

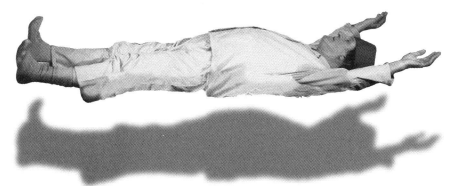

STRETCH THE LEFT LEG STRAIGHT OUT IN FRONT OF YOU. BRING THE RIGHT LEG UP SHARPLY TO JOIN IT. IF YOU DON'T FALL FLAT ON YOUR BACK, YOU'VE LEARNT TO FLY.

Your assistant in this spectacular stage illusion is seen to be covered with a sheet. Gradually he rises in a trance and begins to float around the stage. Then all is revealed and amazement gives way to laughter.

This is a perfect example of a magic trick where the secret is even more entertaining than the initial effect. For that reason, it has found its way into the repertoire of many clown troupes over the years. In fairness, no serious magician would hope to get away with it!

It all costs no more than a modest outlay at your local hardware shop. Get two long poles or broomsticks about the height of the person to be levitated and fix the ends to two shoes. The illustration shows you how the subject needs to be positioned beneath the sheet before the curtain goes up. The working will be obvious.

Once the body has risen into the air, the magician manages to get the corner of the sheet caught beneath his foot. The sheet falls away to produce one of the funniest laughs in magic – burlesque conjuring in the best Tommy Cooper tradition.

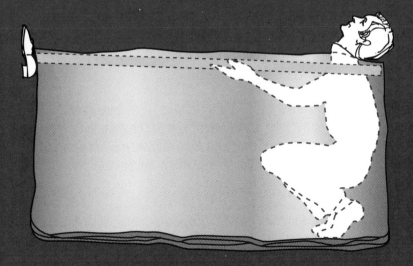

THE WORLD FAMOUS SHIRT TRICK

THE HAND IS QUICKER THAN THE EYE - THAT'S WHY YOU SEE SO MANY BLACK EYES!

Ethically speaking magicians shouldn't use stooges. That said, there can be no harm in resorting to such tactics in the cause of harmless fun.

This is just about the most famous of the stunts that could hardly be worked any other way. It is also the gag Tommy attempted – hilariously – to work on his unrelated namesake, the boxer Henry Cooper, on one of his television shows.

Unfastening the buttons of the shirt at the neck and the cuffs, the magician grabs the back of the collar and pulls. The shirt is supposed to come away completely.

Ahead of the show your accomplice needs to put the shirt on in a special way. The illustrations show how the shirt is draped over his back like a cloak with the sleeves hanging loose. The collar is buttoned and a tie can be worn in the conventional manner. Likewise the cuffs are fastened around the wrists as usual, but leaving the sleeves free of the arms. However, when he puts a jacket on over the shirt, all will appear quite normal. Simply take off his tie, undo the buttons and pull. Off comes the shirt!

FRUITY COOPER

I WAS IN THE POST OFFICE THE OTHER DAY - I'D JUST DROPPED IN TO SEE IF MY MARRIAGE LICENCE HAD LAPSED - AND IN FRONT OF ME IN THE QUEUE WAS THIS FELLOW WITH A MASK ON HIS HEAD - HOLDING A BANANA. I SAID TO HIM, 'THAT'S A BANANA.' HE SAID, 'OH, NO! I'VE EATEN MY GUN!'

Offer someone a bowl of fruit. They'll be amazed when they peel their banana to find that it's already sliced or to discover that the apple is already cut into segments.

To prepare the banana you need a needle. Pierce the banana at a dark blemish along one edge and push it through until it reaches the start of the skin on the opposite side. Use a gentle wriggling motion to and fro inside the skin to separate the flesh at that level. Just make sure you do not unnecessarily enlarge the hole made by the needle. Repeat this process two more times at regular points along the banana so that when unzipped the cut segments will appear at regular intervals.

The apple requires a slightly more sophisticated approach. Thread the needle with a length of strong thread, and then sew around the apple just beneath the skin, inserting the needle each time at the exit point of the previous stitch. Make sure you start and finish as near the stem as possible, where you cross the ends of the thread and pull smartly until the many-sided loop comes free. This slices the apple into two halves. To divide the apple into quarters repeat the process at right angles to the first cut. As with the banana, if the process is done neatly, the blemishes left by the needle are hardly distinguishable and should merge into the general texture of the peel.

Expect strange looks when the fruit is peeled and don't expect anyone to want to eat it afterwards!

MORE ONE-LINERS

IF YOU BELIEVE IN THE POWER OF TELEKINESIS, THEN RAISE MY HAND!

THEY ALWAYS SAY, 'PAY YOUR TAXES WITH A SMILE' - BUT THEN THEY INSIST ON CASH!

MY MOTHER ALWAYS TOLD ME I WAS UNIQUE, JUST LIKE EVERYONE ELSE!

I WAS WOKEN UP BY A TAP ON THE DOOR THIS MORNING. I MUST GET THE PLUMBER TO TAKE IT OFF.

DO YOU LIKE BATH BUNS? I DON'T - THE CRUMBS CLOG UP THE PLUGHOLE.

DID YOU HEAR ABOUT THE PSYCHIATRIST WHO CERTIFIED HIMSELF INSANE? HE MADE A FOOL OF HIMSELF!

A LOT OF YOU MAY THINK THAT HYPNOTISM COMES FROM THE MIND. IT DOESN'T. IT COMES FROM THE HIPS!

TWO MIND READERS MET IN THE STREET - ONE SAID, 'YOU'RE FINE. HOW AM I?'

A MEMORY TRICK
(HOW'S YOUR MEMORY?)

I HAVE A PHOTOGRAPHIC MEMORY. THE TROUBLE IS
I FORGET TO REMOVE THE LENS CAP!

This couldn't be simpler and will take no time at all. All you have to
do is memorise these three cards.

When you have done that, say their values out loud a few times. And then
turn the page.

Say that again. 'The Four of Clubs, the Ace of Diamonds and the Two of Spades.' You lose. You shouldn't jump to conclusions. The centre card is the Ace of Hearts!

MY MEMORY'S TERRIBLE. I CUT MYSELF SHAVING TODAY AND I FORGOT TO BLEED!

COOPER'S PATENT ALARM CLOCK

I GOT UP LATE THIS MORNING. I'D SET THE ALARM FOR SEVEN - BUT THERE ARE EIGHT OF US IN THE HOUSE.

For this piece of visual nonsense Tommy displayed seven or eight candles, set up in a row on a table. Each was cut to a different length, starting at around two inches and going up to full size. He explained that each candle would burn for a different length of time.

The illustration will give you an idea

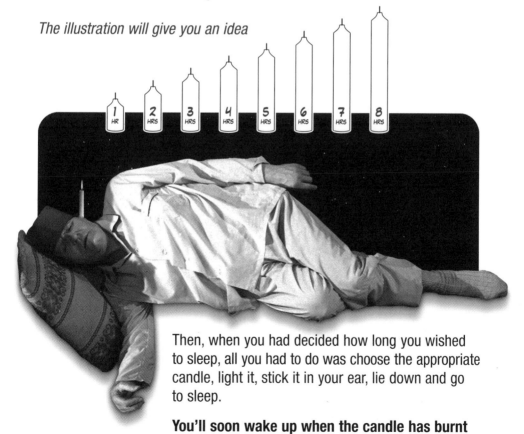

Then, when you had decided how long you wished to sleep, all you had to do was choose the appropriate candle, light it, stick it in your ear, lie down and go to sleep.

You'll soon wake up when the candle has burnt itself out – *just like that!*

GOURMET COOPER

I WENT INTO A RESTAURANT THE OTHER DAY. THE WAITER SAID, 'WHAT'LL YOU HAVE?' I SAID, 'WHAT'S THE FISH LIKE?' HE SAID, 'I DON'T KNOW. I HAVEN'T ASKED IT!'

I SAID TO THE WAITER, 'DO YOUR CHEFS DO BAKED POTATOES IN THEIR JACKETS?' HE SAID, 'NO - THEY DO THEM IN THE OVEN.'

HE SAID, 'WOULD YOU LIKE BREAKFAST IN BED?' I SAID, 'NO. I'LL HAVE IT ON A PLATE!'

I ORDERED A GIN AND VODKA WITH GARLIC - THE GARLIC TELLS THE WAITER WHICH TABLE YOU'RE UNDER!

I ORDERED A HOT CHOCOLATE AND THE WAITER BROUGHT ME A BOX OF MATCHES AND A MARS BAR!

I ASKED THE WAITER FOR A SUGGESTION. HE SAID, 'WELL, I WOULDN'T WEAR THAT COLOUR TIE WITH THAT SHIRT.'

YOU SHOULD HAVE SEEN THIS PERSON AT THE NEXT TABLE. TALK ABOUT BAD MANNERS. I DON'T MIND ANYBODY EATING WITH THEIR HANDS, BUT SOUP?

IT WAS A MARVELLOUS RESTAURANT. MARVELLOUS. AND I WAS SO HUNGRY - I WAS STARVING. I ATE EVERYTHING ON THE MENU. WELL, THEY DIDN'T HAVE ANY PLATES!

THEY'VE GOT A SPECIALITY THAT MELTS IN THE MOUTH. ICE CREAM!

SEE-THROUGH COOPER

> MY WIFE HAS X-RAY VISION.
> SHE CAN SEE THROUGH EVERYTHING!

Few optical illusions are more surprising than this one. Roll a piece of paper into a tube about an inch in diameter and fasten it with an elastic band. This becomes your magic telescope. Hold one end to your right eye with your right hand and then hold your left hand – the palm facing you – against the tube as in the illustration.

Adjust your focus so that you are looking through the tube with your right eye and concentrate upon your left hand with your left eye. If you are doing things correctly, a hole will mysteriously appear in your hand – indeed you will be able to see objects beyond the hole. Sometimes it is hard to believe what our eyes tell us, but have no doubts about this trick.

TOPSY-TURVY MONEY

I'VE FOUND THAT THE BEST WAY TO DOUBLE YOUR MONEY IS TO FOLD IT IN HALF - AND PUT IT IN YOUR POCKET!

This trick requires a little practice, but once mastered it will baffle anybody who sees it. In effect, you cause a banknote – denomination is irrelevant – to turn itself upside down in your hands by magic.

It is simply a matter of following the folding instructions set out in the illustrations.

1. Hold a note the correct way up in your left hand as shown

2. Then fold the bottom long edge up and forwards to the top edge.

3. Fold the right-hand side of the note back behind the left-hand side.

4. Finally fold the right-hand side forward in front of the left-hand side. The result will be as shown in the illustration. Here pause and emphasise that at no point has the note been turned upside-down and challenge anyone to shout if they see anything suspicious happen as you unfold the money.

5 & 6. Now unfold the note just as if you were turning over the pages of a book from left to right.

7. When you reach this stage fold the front top edge down towards you and the note will be upside down, even though you did not obviously turn it over.

It helps if you have a note in your wallet that already has the creases in it beforehand.

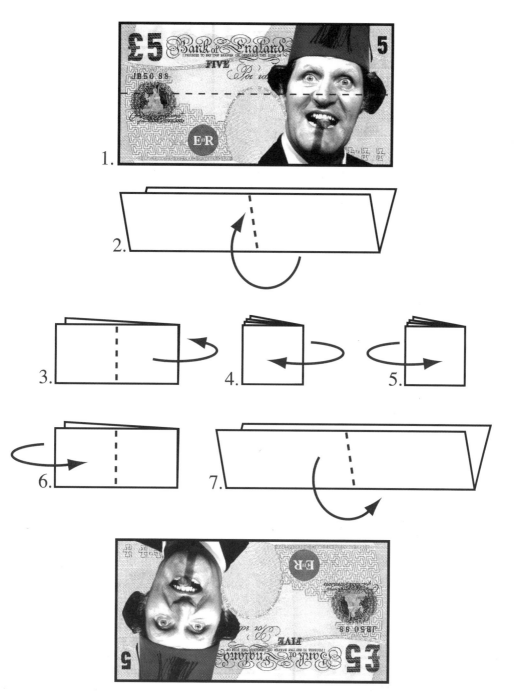

THE INVISIBLE HAIR

MY AGENT IS SENSITIVE ABOUT HIS HAIR - WHICH IS ODD, BECAUSE HE DOESN'T HAVE ANY!

Tommy's miming skill was such that when he performed this you would swear you could see the hair. All you need is a large men's handkerchief or table napkin. The stiffer it is, so much the better. Take the centre of the handkerchief in your right hand and pull it up through your left fist as shown, letting it stay upright when about six inches protrude above. Now pretend to pluck an imaginary hair from your head with your other hand and pretend to attach the end to the tip of the handkerchief. All you need to do is just appear to pinch them together. You then pretend to pull the invisible hair down to the right and the handkerchief bends across in the same direction as if it really were attached. When the right hand moves back, the handkerchief is pulled back too.

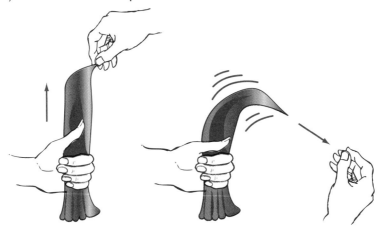

What causes the handkerchief to move back and forth is the secret movement of the left thumb. Just raise and lower it against the cloth. The audience will not see this from the front. Obviously the illusion depends upon coordinating the movements of the handkerchief with those of the right hand. Carry out the effect a few times and then – with the handkerchief pulled over as far as possible to the right – bend forward and pretend to bite through the thread with your teeth. At the precise moment move the left thumb up again and the handkerchief springs back up.

BACK IN THE JUNGLE

SO THIS LION - YOU SEE - WAS STROLLING THROUGH THE JUNGLE AND HE CAME ACROSS THIS ELEPHANT. WELL IT WOULD, WOULDN'T IT? AND HE SAID TO HIM - 'TELL ME,' HE SAID, 'I WAS READING IN THE PAPER THE OTHER DAY THAT ELEPHANTS ALL GO TO THE SAME PLACE - WHAT THEY CALL THE ELEPHANTS' GRAVEYARD - TO DIE. IS THAT TRUE?'

SO THE ELEPHANT SAID, 'THAT'S TRUE. WHEREVER YOU'VE READ IT, THAT'S TRUE. AS A MATTER OF FACT, I'M ON MY WAY THERE NOW.' SO THE LION SAID, 'BUT IS IT TRUE THAT NOBODY HAS EVER DISCOVERED WHERE THE ELEPHANTS' GRAVEYARD IS? THEY'VE LOOKED FOR HUNDREDS OF YEARS AND NEVER FOUND OUT WHERE IT IS?' SO THE ELEPHANT SAID, 'THAT'S TRUE, LION. NOBODY HAS EVER DISCOVERED WHERE THE ELEPHANTS' GRAVEYARD IS.'

SO THE LION SAID, 'IF I FOLLOW YOU, I'LL FIND OUT BECAUSE YOU'RE GOING THERE TO DIE RIGHT NOW - AREN'T YOU? SO THE ELEPHANT SAID, 'NO. YOU'LL NEVER DO THAT. NEVER. BECAUSE THE ELEPHANTS' GRAVEYARD MIGHT BE THERE - OR IT MIGHT BE OVER THERE - OR IT MIGHT BE A LITTLE BIT MORE OVER THERE. BUT WE ELEPHANTS ALWAYS WALK THOUSANDS OF MILES BEFORE WE GET THERE.'

AND THE LION SAID, 'WHY DO YOU DO THAT, JUST TO GO AND DIE?' AND THE ELEPHANT SAID, 'WELL, IT'S THE WALK THAT KILLS US!'

"I'VE HEARD THAT ALCOHOL MAKES YOU FAT, BUT I THINK IT MAKES YOU LEAN. LEAN AGAINST THE BAR, LEAN AGAINST THE WALL, LEAN AGAINST THE FLOOR!"

BACK AT THE BAR

Here's another round of intriguing catches that should keep your hands out of your pockets when it comes to settling up for a round of drinks.

- You have a shot glass full to the brim of whisky and another full of water. Challenge someone to make the two liquids change places using only a playing card.

- Stand six glasses in a line so that the first three are full of liquid and the last three are empty. This time challenge someone to arrange the glasses so that they alternate full and empty, but – and here is the catch – they can move only one glass!

- Take four matches and arrange them as shown. This represents a glass. Then take a coin and place it accordingly. This denotes the cherry. The bet is to move two matches in such a way that the cherry ends up outside the glass. You must not touch the cherry and must make sure that the glass stays in the same shape.

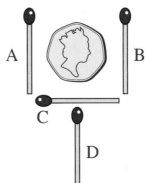

- You have a full glass of beer in front of you. You tell everyone that you are going to make the beer disappear under impossible conditions. You intend to walk out of the room and when you walk back the contents of the glass will have gone. No one else is allowed to touch the glass in any way.

Some of these methods may sound cheeky – one is founded on scientific principles – but all comply with the conditions imposed.

• You must make sure that each glass is full to the brim. Place the playing card on top of the glass of water and turn the glass over holding the card in place. Place the card and glass together over the other glass, trapping the card between the two glasses. The rims of the two glasses must be in exact alignment. Then very carefully edge the card towards you without disturbing the glasses, creating a small opening between the whiskey and the water. After a minute or two the whiskey and the water will have changed places due to the greater density of the water. The stunt will also work using red wine.

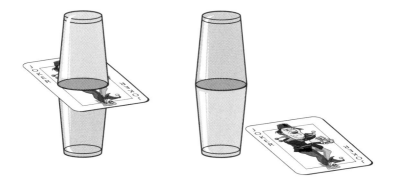

• The solution here is not as complex as it first seems. Pick up the second glass from the left and pour its contents into the second glass from the right. Then make sure you remember to put the new empty glass back where it was!

- The sneaky thing here is that while two matches are moved, in fact the moves could be interpreted as one and a half. First slide C halfway along to the left. Then bring B down to the end of C, as shown. The cherry is now outside the glass. Nothing was said about turning the glass upside down in the process!

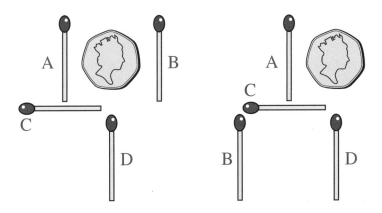

- Having established your bet, you walk out of the room, get down on your hands and knees, crawl back in, make your way to the bar, reach for the beer, down the contents, crawl out again, stand up and – if you still have the stamina – walk back into the room!

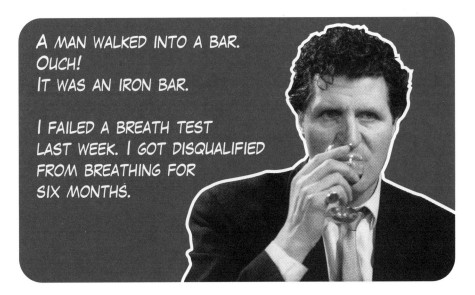

A MAN WALKED INTO A BAR.
OUCH!
IT WAS AN IRON BAR.

I FAILED A BREATH TEST
LAST WEEK. I GOT DISQUALIFIED
FROM BREATHING FOR
SIX MONTHS.

SPOOKY COOPER

LAST EVENING AT A SÉANCE,
I HAD A DREADFUL FRIGHT!
I SAW A POLTERGEI ...
A GEISTERPOL ...
A THING THAT WENT BUMP
IN THE NIGHT!
SAID A GROANING VOICE
FROM 'NEATH THE SHEET,
'THERE'S ONLY THEE
AND ME!'
I SAID, 'GIVE ME MY HAT
AND COAT, AND THERE'LL
BE ONLY THEE!'

If it is performed convincingly, the people who help you in this gag will feel they are genuinely in the presence of things that go bump in the day – let alone the night.

Stand your victim in the centre of the room, totally isolated from the rest of the company. The stunt will fail if the person can attribute what happens to anyone else present. Then explain that you are going to place your two forefingers on his or her eyes. You demonstrate this by extending the forefingers of both hands and placing them gently on their eyelids, which naturally close as the fingers approach. You do this a few times and the spectator can reopen his or her eyes as your fingers withdraw. This stresses that fact that you are using both your hands in the proceedings.

Once more they are asked to close their eyes, but this time as your forefingers approach, you make a sneaky change. As soon as their eyes are shut, you extend both the first and second fingers of your right hand and place them one on each eye. To the spectator it will feel no different from before. While your right hand is in this position, your other hand is free to cause whatever mischief it likes – tapping the spectator on the back of the neck, pulling a handkerchief out of a pocket, tickling them with a feather. It is important that as soon as you withdraw your right hand the left hand is back in position with its forefinger extended. You immediately retract the second figure of the right hand and the spectator will see exactly what was seen before – namely two forefingers being removed from their eyes.

DID YOU HEAR ABOUT THE GHOST WHO WASN'T ALL THERE? HE CLIMBED OVER WALLS!

A BRICKLAYER'S CONUNDRUM

Here's a simple problem with a practical application. Workmen on a building site would find their task less tiring if they could walk less – if, in fact, they could carry five bricks in each hand instead of one. It is possible, but how?

The answer is simple. Place a brick down on its side, and then balance two more bricks crossways over the ends of the first brick. Than take two more bricks and place those across the ends of the last two. All you do now is reach down into the gap between the bricks and grasp the first brick. Lift this and the other four go with you. Easy when you know how!

THERE WERE TWO FELLOWS BUILDING A HOUSE. ONE OF THEM WAS FIXING PLANKS TO A WALL. HE PICKS UP A NAIL AND HAMMERS IT IN. HE PICKS UP ANOTHER NAIL AND THROWS IT AWAY. HE PICKS UP A NAIL AND HAMMERS IT IN. HE PICKS UP ANOTHER AND THROWS IT AWAY. HE KEEPS THIS UP FOR A WHILE AND FINALLY THE OTHER FELLOW COMES OVER AND ASKS, 'WHY ARE YOU THROWING HALF THE NAILS AWAY?' HE SAYS, 'THEY'RE ALL POINTED AT THE WRONG END.' THE OTHER FELLOW SAYS, 'YOU IDIOT, THEY'RE FOR THE OTHER SIDE OF THE HOUSE!'

PING!

I NEVER DRINK BEFORE A SHOW. IF I DID, MY TRICKS MIGHT
START TO GO RIGHT.

Here's a trick that can't fail, however tipsy you might be at the time. All you need for this nifty little stunt is a wooden safety match and a safety pin. Cut the head off the match. Then find the exact centre of what remains and make a hole at this point. The hole should be large enough for the safety pin to pass through snugly, but not too tightly. Start with a large needle and only insert the safety pin at a later stage, else the match will split.

With the match securely impaled on the pin, hold the arrangement firmly in the left hand between thumb and forefinger as shown. The far half of the match must be below the fixed bar of the pin. Now press down smartly on point A with your right forefinger, flicking it off over the end. The match will appear to pass straight through the metal. In fact, it does a somersault, leaving the end you flick on top of the bar. It all happens so quickly that the eye cannot follow it. It is a perfect illusion.

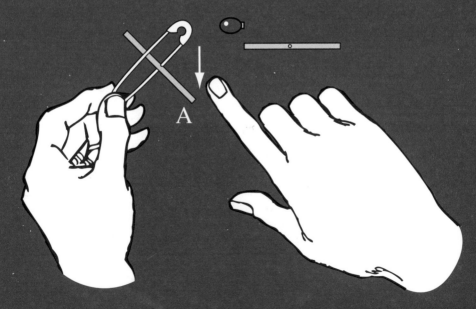

A

MISCHIEVOUS MATCHES

THERE WAS THIS GUY - THEY CALLED HIM PEANUT BRITTLE - HE WAS HALF NUTS!

These stunts aren't all what they seem – in other words, they are not the conventional type of match puzzle!

Start by asking your friend to hold his or her hand in a fist with the knuckles pointing upwards. Take three matches and insert them between the fingers as shown in the illustration. Pretend to concentrate on the exact position of the matches as if you were lining up an extremely difficult feat. Also make a great play of the way the hand should he held – 'up a bit' – 'down a bit' – that sort of thing. Then when everyone is expecting something clever or spectacular to happen, quickly strike another match, light the three matches and start to sing, 'Happy Birthday to You!' Obviously blow them out before they cause any harm.

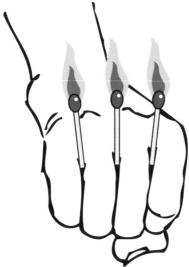

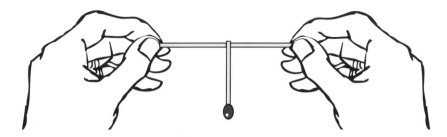

For the second piece of business you again need three matches. Ask somebody to hold two of them together in such a way that they grip the end of the third. It may take a while to get the matches into position exactly, but persevere. Then ask him to scuff one foot on the carpet, even to make a humming sound under his breath. All then is set for the punchline: *'You were born to ride a scooter!'*

Finally insert two matches in the end of a matchbox and ask the victim to hold them between the finger and thumb of each hand. You then explain that he is standing on the runway of a major airport and must listen to the dialogue that takes place between the control tower and the pilot of an aeroplane.

- *'F for Freddie' calling Control Tower. Can you hear me? Over.*

- Control Tower to 'F for Freddie.' I am hearing you loud and clear. Over.

  - *'F for Freddie' calling Control Tower. Asking for permission to land. Over.*

    - Control Tower to 'F for Freddie.' Granting permission to land. Come in. Over.

    - *'F for Freddie' calling Control Tower. Can't possibly land. There's some idiot on the runway with a pram!*

DOWN MEMORY LANE

I'LL NEVER FORGET THE WAR. I FOUGHT WITH THE ARMY. IN THE END I GAVE IN AND JOINED. I GOT THE MILITARY CROSS. MIND YOU, I GOT THE NAVY A BIT ANNOYED AS WELL!

This stunt was popular during the war years – a favourite with entertainers in uniform like Tommy Cooper, who did not have the space to carry loads of apparatus in the standard regulation kitbag.

You need a sheet of paper – A4 size is ideal. This needs to be folded as shown in the illustrations. First bring the bottom shorter edge up and across on a diagonal and crease accordingly. Then halve the triangle so formed by bringing up the point at bottom right – X – to meet the point Y, thus forming another diagonal crease. Finally fold the whole arrangement over upon itself vertically – on an imaginary straight line going through the centre of the chevron.

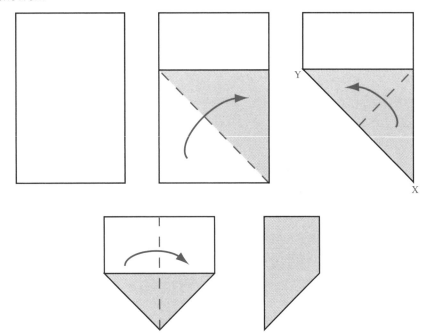

At this point the conjuror in khaki would have started to tell his story, something like this:

Churchill, **Mussolini** and **Hitler** all arrived at the Pearly Gates, to be greeted by St Peter. First Peter said to Mussolini, 'Have you got a ticket.' He replied, 'No' – so Peter tore him off two strips, A and B. The pieces were unfolded and arranged – you demonstrate accordingly – to spell the word HELL.

A & B

Mussolini was despatched downstairs to Hades and then it was Hitler's turn. He didn't have a ticket either, so he was given strip C. When this was unfolded, the pieces were arranged to form a swastika.

C

'That sign is not recognised here,' said Peter and Hitler was sent to Hell also.

Churchill was left with the last ticket. This was all in one piece. When unfolded, it formed a cross. St Peter opened the gates without delay.

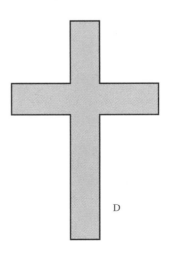

As another famous comedian was known to sing, 'Who do you think you are kidding, Mr Hitler?'

D

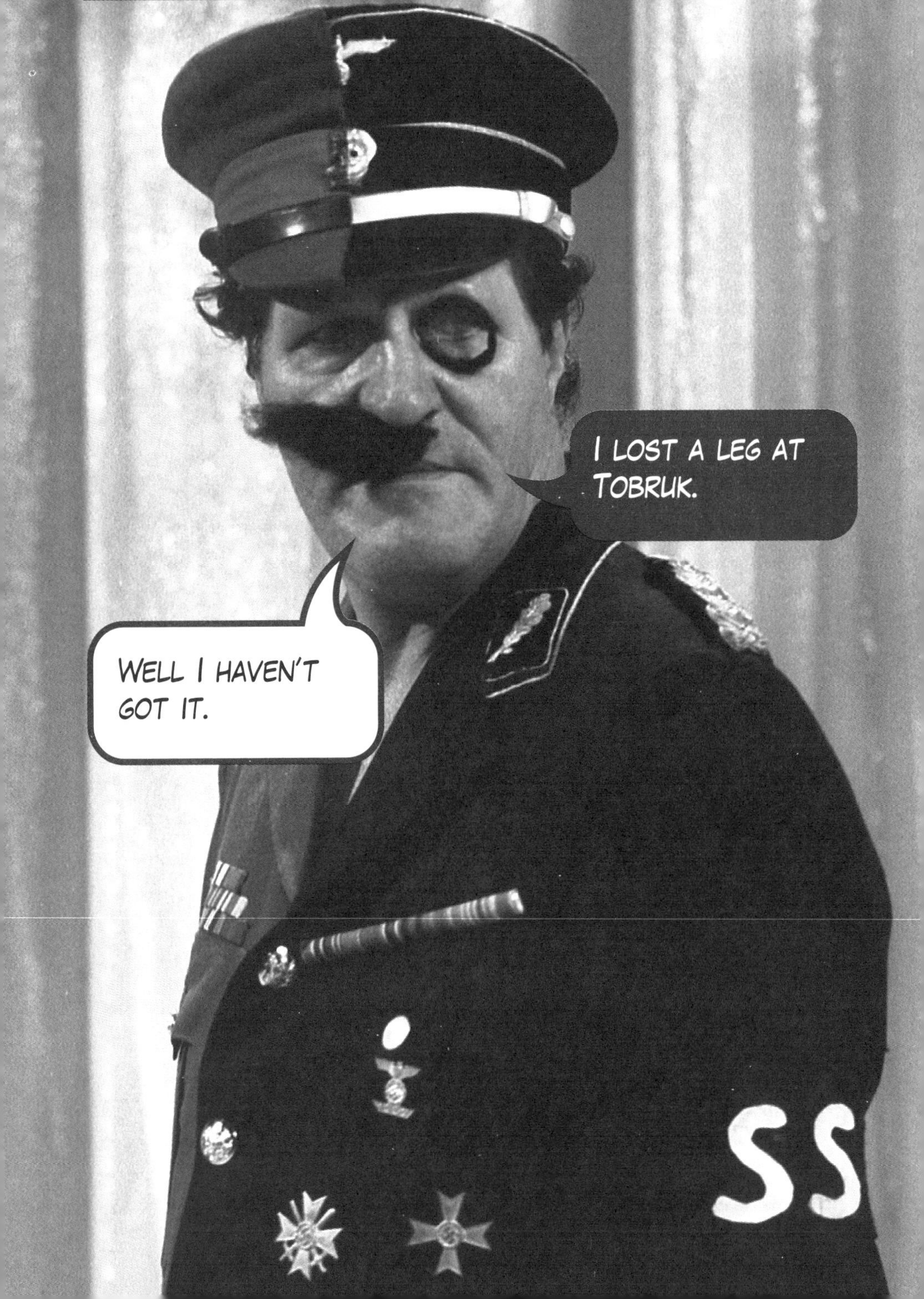
I LOST A LEG AT TOBRUK.
WELL I HAVEN'T GOT IT.
SS

LAUGHTER MISCELLANY THREE

A DUCK WALKED INTO A CHEMIST AND ASKED, 'DO YOU SELL LIP SALVE?' THE MAN BEHIND THE COUNTER SAID, 'YES. HOW DO YOU WANT TO PAY FOR IT?' THE DUCK SAID, 'OH, JUST PUT IT ON MY BILL.'

I WENT TO A SHOE SHOP THE OTHER DAY TO BUY A PAIR OF SLIPPERS. I TRIED A PAIR ON AND THEY FELT JUST RIGHT. I SAID TO THE GIRL, 'WHAT DO YOU THINK?' SHE SAID, 'OH, THEY FIT YOU LIKE A GLOVE.' I SAID, 'GOOD. I'LL TAKE A PAIR OF SHOES TO KEEP MY HANDS WARM.'

I LOVE FISHING - IT RELAXES ME. I WENT FLY FISHING THE OTHER DAY - CAUGHT THREE FLIES. YOU SHOULD HAVE SEEN THE ONE THAT GOT AWAY - IT WAS THIS BIG. (TOMMY HOLDS UP HIS HAND WITH HIS FOREFINGER AND THUMB ABOUT A QUARTER OF AN INCH APART.) IT MUST HAVE BEEN A BLUEBOTTLE!

DID YOU HEAR ABOUT THE CHAP WHO HAD FAIRIES AT THE BOTTOM OF HIS GARDEN? THERE WERE SIX OF THEM. HE USED TO GO DOWN THERE AND COUNT THEM EVERY NIGHT. ONE NIGHT HE WENT DOWN AND HE COUNTED, 'ONE - TWO - THREE - FOUR - FIVE ...' HE WAS A FAIRY LIGHT!

I LOVE ART. TAKE VAN GOGH - WHAT A MARVELLOUS PAINTER - HE CUT OFF HIS EAR AND SENT IT TO HIS GIRLFRIEND, JUST LIKE THAT! AND THEY ALL SAID, 'VAN GOGH IS A GENIUS' AND HE SAID, 'EH?'

HOLDING THE BABIES

A WOMAN WAS ASKED IF HER TWINS MADE A LOT OF NOISE AT NIGHT. SHE SAID, 'I CAN'T BE SURE, BECAUSE ONE OF THEM SCREAMS SO LOUD WE CAN'T HEAR THE OTHER ONE!'

It's hard to imagine a funnier living cartoon than this one. The stunt is best played on a young man, unmarried, one who – you explain – may wish to know what the future holds in store for him. It is best done amongst friends and you'll also need a large white table napkin, two white gentlemen's handkerchiefs, two safety pins and a soluble black magic marker pen.

Ask him to face you with his back to the crowd and tell him to fold his arms, holding the backs of his hands up and outwards. It is best that you guide the hands into position, as you arrange the napkin around his chest and arms, pinning each side tightly to the back of his jacket or shirt. The backs of his hands should be visible above the top of the cloth at the wrists. The illustration explains all. Take the two handkerchiefs and tie them rope-fashion around each hand, to resemble a baby's bonnet. Finally, take the pen and quickly sketch eyes, eyebrows, nose, mouth on the hands.

Ask him to turn around – he won't be able to fathom exactly what you've been doing – but when you explain that this is a vision of his future, there should be laughs all round. Ask him to jiggle his fists slightly up and down and the babies come to life. Have one of those sound effect gizmos that produces baby noises – obtainable in most joke shops – secretly in your pocket to increase the fun.

TOMMY AND THE MAGIC CIRCLE

The President, Francis White, invests Tommy with Membership of The Inner Magic Circle, 15 October 1966.

I'M A MEMBER OF THE MAGIC CIRCLE. I AM ALSO A MEM-
BER OF THE SECRET SIX. IT'S SO SECRET I DON'T EVEN
KNOW THE OTHER FIVE!

Tommy took great pride in his membership of the world's most exclusive magical society. In fact, he was one of the élite admitted eventually to the prestigious Inner Magic Circle. In 1963, when the organisation published a special volume of new tricks dedicated to Lewis Davenport & Company, the long established firm of suppliers of magicians' equipment, the name of Tommy Cooper was prominent amongst the top magicians of the day in the list of contributors. Here is his contribution.

This may not be the best item in the book, but it will be the shortest. Moreover, I can promise you that you can perform it after only a few hours' practice, and that it calls for no duplicate cards, no confederates, and no difficult memorising.

Here are the simple instructions, step by step:

- *Take the Queen of Hearts from a pack of cards (your own or borrowed). Hold it between the first and second fingers of the right hand. Raise the right hand slightly above your head.*

- *Patter as follows: 'This card is now going to be placed completely under my command. It will do anything I tell it to do. I will now demonstrate this.'*

- *At this stage, fling the card boldly into the air and order it to come down again. It will do so every time.**

This trick never fails.

* Unless you throw it too hard, when it may stick to the ceiling if you've got marmalade on your fingers.

THE MAGIC CIRCLE CONSIDERS ME ONE OF THE BEST
MAGICIANS THEY HAVE TURNED OUT. THEY'VE TURNED ME
OUT OF THE CLUBROOM, THE LIBRARY, THE THEATRE ...!

COOPER FOR CHRISTMAS

LOOK AT THOSE FEET. WHY DO YOU THINK I GREW THEM SO BIG? SO THAT I'D GET MORE PRESENTS IN MY SOCKS ON CHRISTMAS DAY.

ONE NIGHT FATHER CHRISTMAS LEFT ME A NOTE SAYING NOT TO CHEAT BY PUTTING MY FATHER'S SOCK OUT INSTEAD OF MY OWN ... AND IT WAS MINE!

MIND YOU, I'M SO TALL THERE'S SNOW ON MY FEZ ALL THE YEAR ROUND.

I'LL NEVER FORGET THE CHRISTMAS I WENT DOWN WITH A BAD BACK. I HAD TO HAVE ACUPUNCTURE AND I KNEW IT WAS CHRISTMAS BECAUSE THEY USED HOLLY INSTEAD OF PINS.

WHEN WE WERE YOUNG, WE WERE SO POOR THAT ONE CHRISTMAS MY FATHER WENT OUT INTO THE BACKYARD WITH HIS SHOTGUN. THERE WAS A LOUD BANG AND HE CAME BACK IN AND SAID, 'SORRY, KIDS, I'VE HAD TO SHOOT SANTA CLAUS.'

ACTUALLY THERE WAS ONE THING ABOUT CHRISTMAS. WITH MY DAD BEING A POULTRY FARMER - HE REALLY WAS - WE NEVER WENT SHORT OF CHICKENS AND TURKEYS. IN FACT, WE GOT SICK OF THEM. THE LUXURIES WERE THE VEGETABLES. MY FATHER WOULD SAY GRACE AND WHEN WE LOOKED UP HE'D EATEN THEM ALL.

THINGS GOT SO BAD THAT MY MOTHER USED TO PUT IOUS IN THE CHRISTMAS PUDDING INSTEAD OF SIXPENNY BITS.

ONE THING I LOVE ABOUT CHRISTMAS IS THE PANTOMIME. I WAS IN *ROBINSON CRUSOE* ONCE. I PLAYED HIS MANSERVANT, SHEFFIELD WEDNESDAY.

THE NEXT YEAR I PLAYED IN *ALADDIN*. I TOUCHED THE LAMP AND THE GENII APPEARED. ONE NIGHT I TOUCHED JEANNIE AND HER HUSBAND APPEARED!

AT CHRISTMAS TIME OUR HOME IN CHISWICK IS OPEN HOUSE TO EVERYONE ... BECAUSE WE CAN'T AFFORD A FRONT DOOR!

WE LIKE TO HAVE OUR NEIGHBOURS AND FRIENDS IN FOR A DRINK. WHAT'S WRONG WITH THAT? WATER'S FREE, ISN'T IT?

LAST YEAR WE HAD THIS REALLY FINE BIRD - PLUCKED IT AND STUFFED IT WITH SAGE AND ONION. THIS YEAR WE REALLY MUST GET AROUND TO KILLING AND EATING THE THING.

MY WIFE NORMALLY POURS ALL SORTS OF DRINK OVER OUR TURKEY - BRANDY, SCOTCH, GIN, RUM. THE MEAT TASTES AWFUL, BUT YOU SHOULD TAKE A SIP OF THE GRAVY!

THEN THERE'S ALWAYS THE FRIEND WHO SENDS YOU THE JOKE PRESENT. ONE YEAR SOMEONE GAVE US THIS STRANGE LITTLE GREEN DOG - ALL LOW TO THE GROUND, IT WAS, AND FIERCE. IT WASN'T UNTIL IT HAD EATEN THREE KENNELS, SEVERAL STRAY TOMCATS AND A COUPLE OF DUSTMEN THAT WE REALISED IT WAS A CROCODILE.

IT NEVER FAILS!

This may well be the wildest prediction you will ever experience. You will need an ordinary die (or dice) – and a flat surface.

- First imagine a pack of cards – there are four suits – hearts, diamonds, spades and clubs. Say out loud the one that jugglers juggle.

- Now take the dice and roll it on the table until it stops.

- The dice will determine the card you will choose. Here's how.

- Remember the number of spots on the top of the dice.

- Now lift the dice and note the number of spots on the opposite side against the table top.

- Add the two numbers together.

- Now divide the number by two.

- Say out loud the number.

- Say out loud the suit and the number together.

- Wouldn't it be amazing if they matched the prediction over the page?

TOMMY'S MAD HOUSE

THE OTHER DAY I CAME HOME AND THE WIFE WAS CRYING HER EYES OUT. I SAID, 'WHAT ARE YOU CRYING FOR?' SHE SAID, 'I'M HOMESICK.' I SAID, 'THIS IS YOUR HOME.' SHE SAID, 'I KNOW AND I'M SICK OF IT!'

Around the house Tommy Cooper was an inveterate practical joker – even to the extent of sitting life-size ventriloquists' dummies on the loo seat. When you have graduated from the idea of leaving imitation spiders in the bath or on the breakfast tray, you might wish to progress to wheezes like these. They are guaranteed to bring panic and mayhem to the most controlled domestic environment and, although they are not conjuring tricks as such, all of them – like the best magic – set out to prove that nothing is as it seems.

You can begin by creating the illusion of a nasty tear in the wallpaper by taking a small piece of paper about five inches square. Newspaper is ideal, but obviously you have to search the paper for a piece without print. If not, it will work with any piece of plain lightweight paper without a shiny surface. Fold it in two and tear out a long triangular piece as shown in the first illustration. Then crinkle one side as in the second picture, making sure that it curls round slightly. Moisten the back of the other side with the tip of your tongue and stick it in an eye-catching position on a wall with wallpaper on it. Watch the owner of the house when he or she sees the 'tear'. Just make sure you don't use paste or glue to stick the torn piece in place.

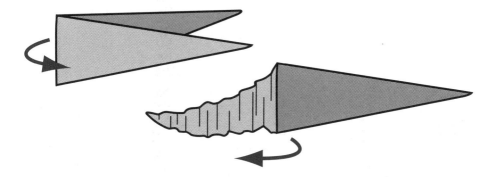

To achieve the next scare, move along to the bathroom. Unscrew the shower head and wipe it dry. Then insert an Oxo cube. You may have to crumble this slightly to make it fit. Screw the shower head back into position. You won't be there when the victim of this prank gets the shock of his life, but he's likely to spend the rest of the day smelling of beef extract and pondering why the water was so disgustingly discoloured.

While in the bathroom you could also cut a short section off the end of an empty toothpaste tube and refill it with peanut butter. Insert as much as you can with a spoon and use a desk stapler to reseal the end. If you curl the end over a few times no one will notice. Don't expect an immediate reaction because there will be a residue of normal toothpaste to be squeezed out first, but in time white or pink – or whatever – will turn to brown and send the first user rushing to the mouthwash.

Finally make your way to the kitchen and take an unopened carton of milk or fruit juice from the fridge. Use a sharp instrument to make a puncture halfway down the side. No milk or juice will trickle out, until the carton is opened or the cap is unscrewed. Just make sure that no one slips on the puzzling wet surface that ends up on the floor.

Cooper's Helpful Hints

To prevent milk from boiling over, keep it in the cow!

To ensure a very soft-boiled egg, just dip it in boiling water for a second.

Ink stains can be removed from a white tablecloth - with a pair of sharp scissors!

To make butter go a long way - send it to South America!

A cure for insomnia? Sleep on the edge of the bed - you'll soon drop off!

A word of advice? Never spit in a man's face - unless his moustache is on fire!

And always put your best foot forward, especially when walking in the dark!

The best way to prevent rice sticking together is to cook each grain separately!

The best way to keep down your bills is to use this - a heavier paperweight!

I'd also like to recommend this. It's a blue banana. It's for people with yellow jaundice - to stop them eating their fingers by mistake.

EAT A LIVE TOAD FIRST THING IN THE MORNING – THEN NOTHING WORSE CAN HAPPEN TO YOU FOR THE REST OF THE DAY!

THE TROUBLE WITH OWNING YOUR OWN HOME – NO MATTER WHERE YOU SIT, YOU'RE LOOKING AT SOMETHING THAT HAS TO BE DONE.

BEFORE CRITICISING PEOPLE WALK A MILE IN THEIR SHOES. THEN WHEN YOU DO CRITICISE THEM, YOU'LL HAVE A MILE START AND YOU'LL HAVE THEIR SHOES!

FINALLY, DO FLIES BOTHER YOU? I WOULDN'T HARM A FLY. I WON'T EVEN SPRAY THEM WITH FLY-KILLER. I USE THIS. *(TOMMY PICKS UP AN AEROSOL CAN AND SPRAYS THE AIR.)* INSTANT STARCH! IT DOESN'T KILL THEM – BUT YOU SHOULD SEE THEM GLIDE OUT THE WINDOW LIKE THAT! *(TOMMY DEMONSTRATES WITH HIS ARMS HELD OUT LIKE A GLIDER.)*

INCIDENTALLY, IF A FLY HAD NO WINGS, WOULD YOU CALL IT A WALK?

OH, JACK, AFTER ALL THOSE YEARS AT SEA, CAN IT REALLY BE YOU?'
NO - MY NAME'S FRED!

EGG, BAG - BAG, EGG

I WOULD LIKE TO SHOW YOU NOW THE VERY FAMOUS EGG AND BAG TRICK. HERE IS THE EGG AND HERE IS THE BAG.

NOW I WANT YOU TO WATCH ME VERY, VERY CLOSELY AND IF YOU SEE ANY SUSPICIOUS MOVES, DON'T SAY ANYTHING. THIS EGG WILL NOW VANISH IN FRONT OF YOUR VERY EYES AND YOU WON'T HAVE THE SLIGHTEST IDEA WHERE IT HAS GONE.

ON THE OTHER HAND I HAVE FOUR FINGERS AND A THUMB - OH DEAR!

I SHALL MAKE THE EGG VANISH IN FRONT OF YOUR VERY EYES.

LOOK, VANISHED IN FRONT OF YOUR VERY EYES AND YOU HAVEN'T THE SLIGHTEST IDEA WHERE IT HAS GONE, HAVE YOU?

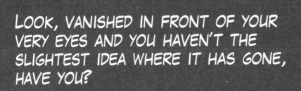

WHERE? UNDER MY ARM? NO!

THE OTHER ONE? NO!

WHAT THIS ONE? NO!

HIGHER? HOW ABOUT THAT!

THANK YOU VERY MUCH. AND YOU PUT YOUR HAND INSIDE THE BAG AND YOU BRING THE EGG OUT TO THUNDEROUS APPLAUSE - YOU BRING THE EGG OUT TO THUNDEROUS APPLAUSE ...

... IT'S NOT MY NIGHT, IS IT? I'VE ALWAYS BEEN UNLUCKY. I HAD A ROCKING HORSE ONCE AND IT DIED!

TRAMPS & CHICKENS

MAGIC! WHAT I DON'T KNOW ABOUT MAGIC WOULD FILL AN AIRCRAFT HANGAR!

This is a classic conjuring stunt that is a trick and a puzzle at the same time. You need seven small objects that must all look the same – coins or matches are perfect. Let's assume you're using coins. Five coins represent the chickens and two coins the tramps. Your hands represent two barns. Have the chickens arranged in a row of five, with the two tramps underneath.

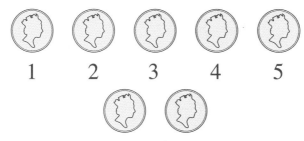

There were these two tramps. They hadn't eaten for days. They arrived at this farmyard, which had chickens running about all over the place. The tramps – they each hid in a barn (Pick up one of the lower two coins in the left hand and the other in the right) and when the coast was clear ...

the first tramp took a chicken into his barn

(Pick up coin 1 in your left hand),

the second tramp took a chicken into his barn

(Pick up coin 5 in your right hand),

the first tramp took another chicken

(Pick up coin 2 in your left hand),

the second tramp took the next chicken

(Pick up coin 4 in your right hand),

and the first tramp took the last one

(Pick up coin 3 in your left hand).

Just as they were about to leave they heard the farmer coming, so they quickly returned the chickens to the farmyard. (You now put the coins back in a row – one at a time – starting with the right hand. That should leave you with no coins in your right and two in your left, although the audience will think you have one coin in each hand.)

The farmer looked round, saw the five chickens were safe and left. The tramps wasted no time in springing into action and took the chickens back. (Pick up the five coins as before – alternating one at a time – beginning with the left hand.)

The farmer became suspicious and came back with a policeman. But when they looked inside the barns they found all five chickens in one barn and two old tramps sleeping in the other – just like that!

At this point you open your left hand to show the five coins – the chickens, and then the right to reveal the other two – the tramps. You can fool yourself performing this trick, but don't be tempted to go stealing chickens.

I CAN DO TRICKS.
IT'S JUST THAT WHEN
I GET IN FRONT OF
AN AUDIENCE THINGS
HAPPEN TO ME.
LIKE FEAR!

A DOVE STORY

NOW FROM THIS EMPTY BAG I SHALL PRODUCE A REAL LIVE DOVE.

I ALWAYS HIT THAT BAG TOO HARD!

LAUGHTER MISCELLANY FOUR

SO I GOT HOME THE OTHER NIGHT AND THE PHONE WAS RINGING. I PICKED IT UP AND SAID, 'WHO'S SPEAKING?' AND A VOICE SAID, 'YOU ARE!'

I HAD A HAIRCUT LAST WEEK. NEXT WEEK I'M GOING BACK TO HAVE ANOTHER ONE CUT. MY BARBER'S SO QUICK. I WALKED IN, SAT DOWN AND HE SHAMPOOED MY FEZ BEFORE I COULD GET IT OFF!

I SAID TO THE CHAP BEHIND THE COUNTER, 'I WANT SOME ROPE.' HE SAID, 'HOW MUCH.' I SAID, 'HAVE YOU GOT A HUNDRED FEET?' HE SAID, 'WHAT DO YOU THINK I AM – A CENTIPEDE?'

THIS OLD LADY CAME UP TO ME THE OTHER DAY AND SAID, 'EXCUSE ME, YOUNG MAN, BUT DO YOU THINK YOU COULD SEE ME ACROSS THE ROAD?' I SAID, 'I DON'T KNOW, LOVE, BUT I'LL GO ACROSS AND HAVE A LOOK.'

I GOT HOME LATE THE OTHER MORNING AND MY WIFE SAID, 'WHERE HAVE YOU BEEN?' I SAID, 'I'VE BEEN PLAYING GOLF.' SHE SAID, 'GOLF?' I SAID, 'YES, I'VE JUST BEEN AROUND EIGHTEEN HOLES.' SHE SAID, 'HOW DO YOU FEEL.' I SAID, 'GIDDY!'

DID YOU HEAR ABOUT THE TWO AERIALS THAT MET ON A ROOF, FELL IN LOVE AND GOT MARRIED? THE CEREMONY WAS BRILLIANT, BUT THE RECEPTION WAS RUBBISH!

MEET THE WIFE AGAIN

> I HAVE THE TIDIEST WIFE IN THE WORLD. SHE PUTS PAPER UNDER THE CUCKOO CLOCK!

I'VE HAD A FUNNY DAY. I WAS LYING DOWN BY THE FRONT DOOR THIS MORNING WHEN THE WIFE WALKED OUT ON ME!

I KNOW IT ISN'T NICE TO TALK BEHIND HER BACK - BUT IT'S THE ONLY CHANCE I GET!

SHE TREATS ME LIKE A KING. WHENEVER I COME IN LATE, SHE CROWNS ME.

I KNOW A VENTRILOQUIST WHO CAN TALK FOR TEN MINUTES WITHOUT OPENING HIS MOUTH. MY WIFE CAN DO BETTER THAN THAT. SHE CAN TALK ALL DAY WITHOUT ANYTHING TO SAY!

MY WIFE - SHE NEVER STOPS TALKING. SHE'S TALK, TALK, TALK, TALK ALL THE TIME AND I WAS GOING ALONG ON MY MOTORBIKE THE OTHER DAY. SHE'S SITTING AT THE BACK, STILL TALKING - CHATTER, CHATTER, CHATTER - ALL THE TIME. AND I WAS GOING ALONG AND A POLICE CAR STOPPED ME AND I SAID, 'WHAT HAVE I DONE, OFFICER?' AND HE SAID, 'NOTHING, BUT I THOUGHT I OUGHT TO TELL YOU YOUR WIFE FELL OFF TWELVE MILES BACK.' I SAID, 'THANK GOODNESS FOR THAT. I THOUGHT I WAS GOING STONE DEAF!'

ANIMAL CRACKERS

A FRIEND OF MINE LIVES ALONE. JUST HIM AND HIS DOG.
HE SAID TO ME 'HE'S A MARVELLOUS COMPANION. HE DOES
EVERYTHING FOR ME. FETCHES MY SLIPPERS, GETS MY PIPE,
HE'S COMPLETELY FAITHFUL.' I SAID, 'THAT'S ALL VERY WELL,
BUT HAVEN'T YOU EVER THOUGHT OF GETTING MARRIED?'
HE SAID, 'YES, BUT I DON'T THINK THE DOG IS SERIOUS!'

I CAME HOME THE OTHER NIGHT. THE DOG WAS SITTING
QUIETLY IN THE CORNER. THE WIFE WAS WORRIED ABOUT
HIM. SHE SAID, 'HE'S UPSETTING ME LOOKING AT ME LIKE
THAT AND GROWLING. IT'S THOSE BIG, SAVAGE, YELLOW TEETH.'
I SAID 'WELL, TAKE THEM OUT - YOU'RE FRIGHTENING HIM.'

THIS MAN WAS SITTING NEXT TO ME ON AN AEROPLANE.
HE SAID, 'I'VE GOT A PARROT AT HOME THAT SAYS,
"WHO'S A PRETTY BOY THEN? WHO'S A PRETTY BOY?"'
I SAID, 'WELL, WHAT'S SO SPECIAL ABOUT THAT? LOTS OF
PARROTS SAY "WHO'S A PRETTY BOY THEN? WHO'S A PRETTY
BOY?"' HE SAID, 'YES, BUT THIS ONE'S STUFFED!'

I GOT THIS ROPE FROM A CHAP IN THE STREET. HE WAS
WALKING ALONG TRAILING IT BEHIND HIM. I SAID, 'WHAT ARE
YOU DOING?' HE SAID, 'I'M TAKING THE DOG FOR A WALK.'
I SAID, 'WHERE'S THE DOG?' HE SAID, 'HE'S TIRED - HE
STAYED AT HOME!'

I TOOK MY DOG TO THE VET THIS MORNING. I SAID,
'THERE'S SOMETHING WRONG WITH MY DOG. HE WON'T EAT
MEAT. HE'LL ONLY EAT APPLES.' THE VET SAID, 'COX'S
PIPPINS?' I SAID, 'NO - HE COCKS HIS BACK LEG LIKE ALL
OTHER DOGS.'

THE MIND-READING DUCK

Used by the STARS Dickie the Duck

TOMMY COOPER and **ROBERT HARBIN** both feature him !

Effect : Three or more cards are freely selected, and, after they are returned to the pack, it's Dickie's job to find them, and this he does in the most entertainingly and delightful way. He chatters, he bites, he throws away unwanted or wrong cards, he gives the selected ones daintily to the audience, in fact, he is the cutest and cleverest little duck that's ever been seen ! **Entirely Mechanical**, the action is a **Dream**, all the variations described above are there for you to work, and how audiences love it, be they young or old ! For Kiddies you can, of course, use any of the popular children's cards now on general sale. **No sleight of hand.** DICKIE comes to you complete with a terrific routine, PLUS many extra ideas, it's **GREAT ENTERTAINMENT** and fine Mystery, **EASY TO DO.** a feature effect that's **READY TO PUT** into your show—**RIGHT AWAY !** We guarantee that it will be the hit of your Programme. Beautifully made, and finished in High-gloss enamel. It will be the pride of your Show !!   **Price   £3/5/-   postage 3/6**

U.S.A. $13.00.

NOW HERE'S A PACK OF CARDS. NOW I'D LIKE SOMEONE IN THE AUDIENCE - SOMEONE AT RANDOM - MR RANDOM - WOULD YOU THINK OF ANY CARD IN THE PACK, SIR, BUT DON'T TELL ME?

THINK OF ANY CARD, SIR - JUST THINK OF ONE. HAVE YOU THOUGHT OF ONE? RIGHT.

NOW THIS IS A CASE OF MIND OVER MATTER - IF YOU DON'T MIND, I DON'T MATTER!

(TOMMY PICKS UP WOODEN PUPPET DUCK WITH FEED BOX ATTACHED.)

I PUT THE CARDS IN THERE, SIR.

'QUACK, QUACK!!'

NOW THIS DUCK WILL TAKE YOUR CHOSEN CARD FROM THAT PACK.

NOW YOU MAY HAVE
SEEN A DUCK DO THAT
BEFORE - BUT TO BE
FAIR, BLINDFOLDED?

NOW WHAT WAS YOUR
CARD, SIR?

(THE MAN NAMES HIS
CARD.)

CORRECT!

(TOMMY THROWS THE
CARD AWAY)

TOMMY'S REPEAT PRESCRIPTION

This doctor said, 'You'll live to be eighty.'
The fellow said, 'I am eighty.' The doctor said,
'I told you so.'

The matron came in one day and said to me, 'The
specialist's coming in to see you in about ten
minutes. I want you to cheer him up, because he's
very worried about you!'

Then he pumped me full of drugs. I said, 'Do I have
to take this lot?' He said, 'You should be so lucky.
These drugs will make you the most popular man
in the country. Every time you sneeze you cure
somebody.'

I went to my doctor the other day. I said, 'Doctor,
doctor, one of my legs is shorter than the other.
What shall I do?' He said, 'Limp.'

I said, 'Doctor, doctor, I think I'm a burglar.' He
said, 'Have you taken anything for it?'

I said, 'Doctor, doctor, I still think I'm a burglar.'
He said, 'Well take these pills for a week and if
they don't work, I'll have a colour TV.'

I said, 'Doctor, doctor, I feel like a pack of cards.'
He said, 'All right, I'll deal with you later.'

I said, 'Doctor, doctor, I feel like a bridge.' He said,
'What's come over you?' I said, 'Three cars, two
lorries and a motorbike.'

I SAID, 'DOCTOR, DOCTOR, I CAN'T SAY MY Fs, MY Ts OR MY Hs.' HE SAID, 'WELL YOU CAN'T SAY FAIRER THAN THAT.'

I SAID, 'DOCTOR, DOCTOR, I FEEL LIKE I'M AT DEATH'S DOOR.' HE SAID, 'DON'T WORRY - I'LL PULL YOU THROUGH.'

I SAID, 'DOCTOR, DOCTOR, I'VE ONLY GOT FIFTY-NINE SECONDS TO LIVE.' HE SAID, 'JUST STAND OVER THERE A MINUTE.'

NOW HERE'S A JOKE. I CAN'T HELP LAUGHING - I'VE HEARD IT BEFORE. THIS MAN HADN'T BEEN FEELING WELL, SO HE WENT TO THE DOCTOR FOR A CHECK-UP. AFTERWARDS THE DOCTOR CAME BACK WITH THE RESULTS. 'I'M AFRAID I HAVE SOME VERY BAD NEWS. YOU'RE DYING AND YOU DON'T HAVE MUCH TIME LEFT.' 'OH, THAT'S TERRIBLE,' SAID THE MAN. 'HOW LONG HAVE I GOT?' THE DOCTOR SAID, 'TEN ...' THE MAN INTERRUPTED, 'TEN WHAT? MONTHS? WEEKS?' THE DOCTOR CONTINUED, 'NINE ...'

SMOKER'S CORNER

FOR YEARS AND YEARS A CIGARETTE NEVER CROSSED MY LIPS ... AND THEN I LOST MY CIGARETTE HOLDER!

> These first two stunts reveal the inordinate lengths to which the young Tommy Cooper would go to secure a laugh in the free and easy post-war days when smoking was fashionable and political correctness hadn't been born.

'Have a cigarette,' asked Tommy of an innocent victim standing at the bar. He could hardly refuse. Tommy followed with a light. Then very slowly the glow at the end of the cigarette would burn round and round in a spiral until it reached the filter tip. The poor fellow – unsure at first what was happening – would stand there crestfallen with a bedraggled spiral of cigarette paper dangling from his lips, the tobacco scattered all over the floor. Meanwhile Tommy would contentedly puff away at his own smoke. Far from following the fate of the first cigarette, Tommy's burned steadily right through to the end – but with the curious result that the ash appeared to defy gravity.

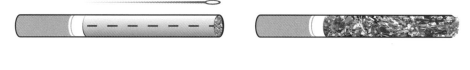

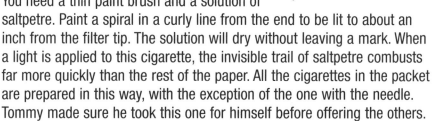

The preparation for the last stunt is simple. Push a long needle through the centre of a cigarette. Anyone can now smoke this without the ash falling off. A little more preparation is needed with the other cigarette. You need a thin paint brush and a solution of saltpetre. Paint a spiral in a curly line from the end to be lit to about an inch from the filter tip. The solution will dry without leaving a mark. When a light is applied to this cigarette, the invisible trail of saltpetre combusts far more quickly than the rest of the paper. All the cigarettes in the packet are prepared in this way, with the exception of the one with the needle. Tommy made sure he took this one for himself before offering the others.

HOWEVER, there are two messages of caution. Always use filter tip cigarettes and never perform over a carpet. That way – no burnt lips and no house fires!

> *I ASKED THE WIFE IF SHE MINDED IF I SMOKED.*
> *SHE SAID SHE DIDN'T CARE IF I BURNED.*

Finally – when people are smoking in your company – amaze them with this little mystery. Borrow a coin and a handkerchief. Wrap the coin in the handkerchief as shown in the illustration. You must make sure that the centre of the cloth is stretched tightly and twisted securely against the flat surface of the coin. Now invite anyone with a lighted cigarette to press the burning end against the flattened centre of the handkerchief. They can hold it there for quite some time. When you take the cigarette away and open the folds of the cloth, the handkerchief will still be intact. There may be a smudge or two of cigarette ash, but no burns or holes as such, although the coin may be very, very hot! Just remember to keep the centre of the handkerchief taut against the coin throughout.

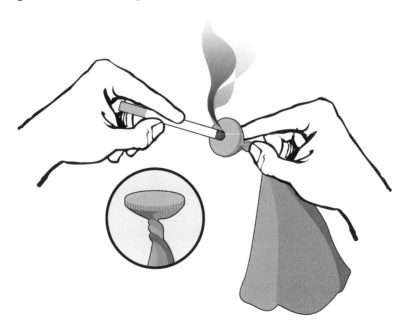

IN A WEEK I SMOKE PACKETS AND PACKETS - NO CIGARETTES, JUST PACKETS!

THE BOTTLE & GLASS TRICK

HERE'S THE VERY FAMOUS BOTTLE AND GLASS TRICK.

HERE'S THE BOTTLE AND HERE'S THE GLASS.

THE BOTTLE WILL NOW CHANGE PLACES WITH THE GLASS.

THE BOTTLE HAS NOW CHANGED PLACES WITH THE GLASS.

THE DIFFICULT PART IS TO MAKE THEM GO BACK AGAIN.

HEY - HOO - WHA - WHA - HOO WHA!

I DON'T KNOW WHAT IT MEANS. I JUST READ IT ON THE BACK OF A TIN OF SARDINES ONCE.

BOTTLE, GLASS!

GLASS, BOTTLE!

BOTTLE, GLASS!
THANK YOU VERY MUCH!

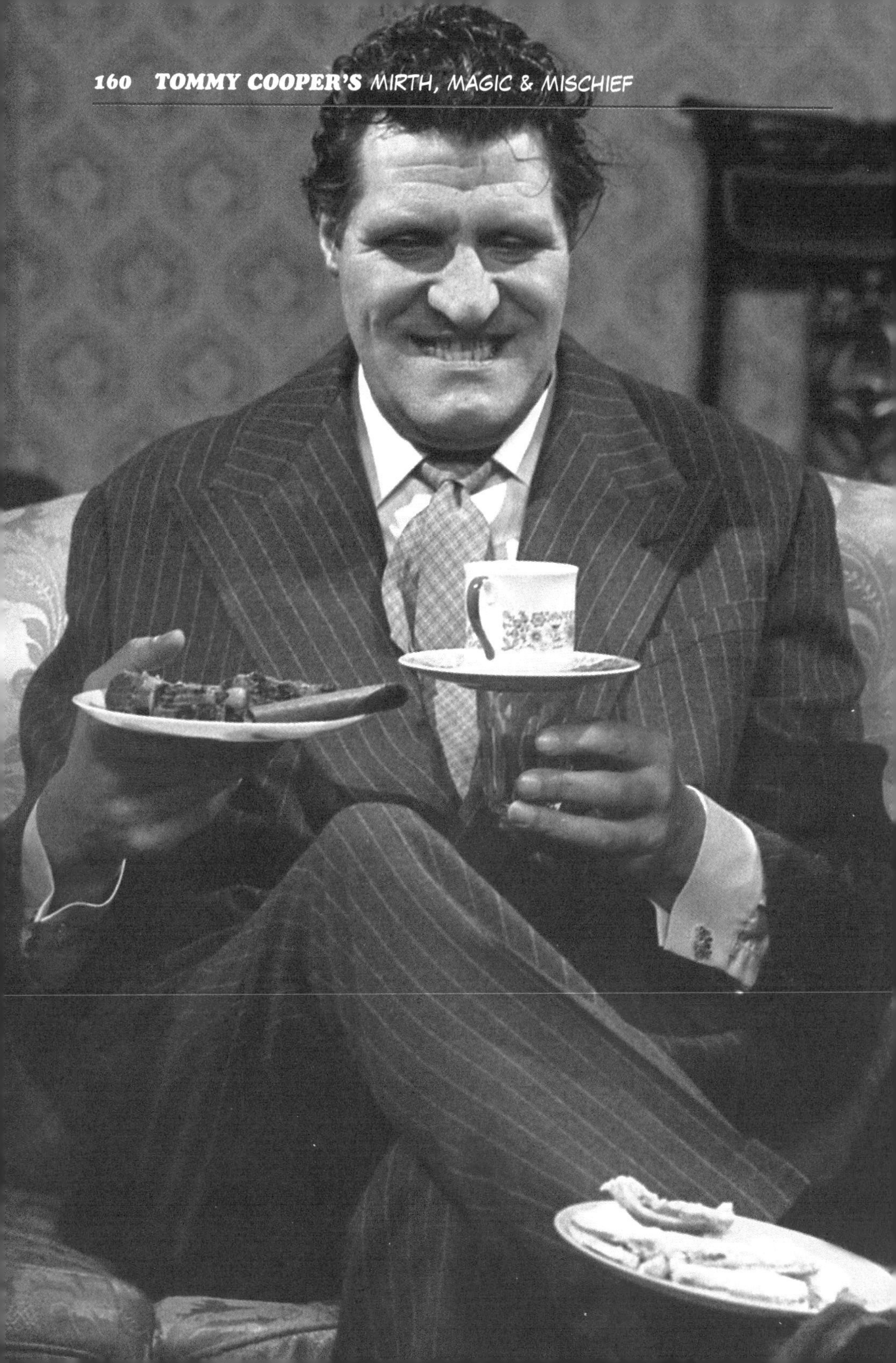

GET OUT OF THAT!

Wait until you're at a party before you try this one and target a victim who needs to be taken down a peg.

You need a broomstick or a long pole. Give this to the fall guy and then fill a glass tumbler almost to the brim with water. Stand on a chair and press the glass against the ceiling. As you have to get down from the chair, ask the fellow to raise the broomstick so that the end keeps the tumbler held in place against the ceiling. Once he has managed this, take the chair away and leave him there! He daren't move for fear of getting a soaking!

HELP!

ACKNOWLEDGEMENTS

I would like to thank Tommy's daughter, Vicky Cooper, and John Miles, on behalf of the Tommy Cooper estate, for their kind support of this project. Special acknowledgement is also made to Ian Adair, Alan Alan, Val Andrews, Eddie Bayliss, Ken Brooke, Gwen Cooper, Henry Cooper, Dana, Devano, Will Dexter, David Drummond, Richard Davies, Bob Dunn, Geoffrey Durham, Peter Eldin, Miff Ferrie, Jerome Flynn, Colin Fox, Martin Gardner, Eddie Gay, Billy Glason, Tommy Godfrey, Robert Harbin, David Hemingway, Peter Hudson, Tudor Jones and the members of the Tommy Cooper Appreciation Society, Mary Kay, William Larsen Senior, Henry Lewis, Trevor Lewis, Clive Mantle, Jay Marshall, Johnnie Mortimer & Brian Cooke, Dell O'Dell, Robert Orben, Patrick Page, Patrick Ryecart, Freddie Sadler, Sirdani, Stuart Snaith and the team at 2entertain, Harry Stanley, Freddie Starr, Eric Sykes, Frankie Vaughan, Willane and Chris Woodward.

Martin Breese was especially gracious in allowing me access to the original advertisements run by Harry Stanley and the 'Unique' Magic Studio, as was Diamond Jim Tyler, of 'Bamboozlers' fame, who opened up for me his vast researches into those areas of impromptu magic and chicanery that have fascinated us both for so long. I thank the Honorary Secretary, David Ball, and Past President, Michael Bailey, for expediting the appropriate permission obtained from The Magic Circle. Special thanks are extended to FremantleMedia for permission to use images from episodes of Tommy's shows produced by Thames Television.

Trevor Dolby, at Preface, had the vision to see how the magic and mirth of Tommy Cooper could again work wonders on the printed page and I extend my gratitude to him and the team at Preface including Nicola Taplin and Neil Bradford. While every effort has been made to trace the owners of copyright material produced herein, the publishers would like to apologise for any omissions and will be pleased to incorporate missing acknowledgements in future editions, provided that notification is made to them in writing.

Working a different kind of wizardry throughout the development of this project has been my designer, Andy Spence. No problem has defeated him as he turned his attention from three-dimensional imagery to precise technical illustration to the basic skill of capturing the magic and showmanship of this great performer in these pages. The major debt I owe to him is matched by what I owe to my representative, Charles Armitage and his associate, Di Evans. Their caring support at tricky times has been especially valuable during the year spent on this project. The loving support of my wife, Sue, once again goes without saying.

JOHN FISHER

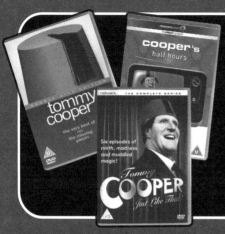